1751

THE SCULPTURE OF FALCONET

> " . . . je n'approuve pas que l'artiste
> se livre à un beau rêve que les spectateurs
> ne pourraient pas faire avec lui."

THE SCULPTURE
OF *Falconet*

BY

GEORGE LEVITINE

with a translation from the French of
Falconet's *Réflexions sur la sculpture* by
EDA MEZER LEVITINE

NEW YORK GRAPHIC SOCIETY LTD.

Greenwich, Connecticut

TO EDA

STANDARD BOOK NUMBER 8212-0383-5
LIBRARY OF CONGRESS CATALOG CARD NUMBER 71-181348

PUBLISHED IN U.S.A. 1972
by New York Graphic Society Ltd.,
GREENWICH, CONNECTICUT

PRINTED IN JAPAN

PREFACE

ANYONE interested in eighteenth-century France is sooner or later faced by Falconet's name. The random reader discovers, for instance, that Falconet was one of the leading sculptors of the reign of Louis XV, that he worked for the Marquise de Pompadour, that he spent some time at the court of Catherine II, and that he corresponded extensively with Diderot. Yet while accumulating, almost unwittingly, a variety of facts about Falconet, one can remain unfamiliar with his work as a sculptor, content to identify it, rather vaguely, as one more illustration of the Rococo style. This situation becomes understandable if one recalls that eighteenth-century French sculpture, unlike French painting, was not rescued from the quicksand of nineteenth-century clichés by the enthusiastic scholarship of the brothers Goncourt. Thus, despite the sculptor's historical and literary prominence, Falconet's name still evokes for many people little more than the music-box nostalgia of Louis Quinze whatnots filled with delicate bronzes, porcelain shepherdesses, elaborate clocks, and erotic marble statuettes. In fact, Falconet was not given serious consideration as an artist until the publication of Hildenbrandt's *Leben, Werke und Schriften des Bildhauers E. M. Falconet* (1908) and, especially, of Réau's *Etienne-Maurice Falconet* (1922).

Since the appearance of these two books — the later one is now almost half-a-century old — there has been a revival of interest in Falconet. But this revival, mainly concerned with Falconet's role in the growth of eighteenth-century philosophical and aesthetic ideas, has had until now little to do with the development of his sculpture, *per se*. The raison d'être of this book is to bring some new light on the major achievements of Falconet as a sculptor.

To fulfill this purpose, it was necessary, of course, to forgo any idea of a systematic consideration of Falconet's writings. Similarly, it was necessary to emphasize the artist's most important works and to omit discussion of many borderline attributions, as well as of some authentic, but decidedly secondary, productions. As far as possible, the study has been organized on a chronological basis. However, a mechanical application of this principle could have created confusion, for the sculptor often explored several stylistic avenues simultaneously. To give a sketch of Falconet's many-sided artistic contribution, it was imperative to evolve an "organic" approach with a good measure of elbowroom to reconcile chronological and thematic points of view.

It is fervently hoped that in the context of the current reinterpretation of the eighteenth century, the present study will attract some attention to the work of one of the most interesting and original sculptors of the French tradition.

The obligations incurred in the writing of this book are many. To the Graduate

5

School of the University of Maryland I owe the assistance that provided me with research funds. To individuals my debts are too wide to be acknowledged adequately. However, I should like to extend my special thanks to the curators and to the staff members of public and private collections who graciously showed me works from their holdings (in many cases not accessible to the public), gave me permission to have these works photographed, and helped me with invaluable information. I am particularly indebted to Mr. Adhémar, Conservateur au Cabinet des Estampes of the Bibliothèque Nationale, Paris; Mlle Baron, Conservateur adjoint au Département des Sculptures of the Louvre Museum; Mlle Brunet, Archiviste-bibliothécaire at the Manufacture Nationale de Céramique of Sèvres; Mlle Burollet, Attachée au Musée Cognac-Jay; Mlle Cornillot, Conservateur des Musées de Besançon; Mr. Fourest, Conservateur au Musée National de Céramique; Mlle Guillaume, Assistante au Musée des Beaux-Arts of Nancy; Mr. Hodgkinson, Keeper, Department of Architecture and Sculpture, Victoria and Albert Museum, and his staff; Mr. Johnston, Assistant Director, and Mr. Randall, Director, of the Walters Art Gallery; and Mme Rocher-Jauneau, Conservateur au Musée des Beaux-Arts of Lyons. Thanks are also due to Mr. Eney, Graduate Assistant at the University of Maryland, who solved many problems pertaining to a number of hitherto unpublished photographs. Finally, I am deeply grateful to my wife, Eda M. Levitine, who helped me at every stage of my research.

CONTENTS

I

The Jean-Jacques of Sculpture

UNUSUALLY self-conscious of his humble origin, Falconet could seldom refrain from flaunting it on most inappropriate occasions. For instance, when he received at the imperial court of Saint Petersburg the title of *highborn*, the sculptor deliberately thumbed his nose at social solemnities, retorting to the Empress in a Figaro-like fashion: "This title befits me remarkably well, since I was born in an attic."[1] This pun was inspired by a fundamental reality. Etienne-Maurice Falconet was born on December 1, 1716, in the *quartier Saint-Denis* — a quarter of Paris always celebrated for its vigorously plebeian character and its earthy folklore.

Falconet was baptized in the church of Saint-Sauveur, and his parents lived in the same *quartier*, rue Bourbon-Villeneuve. His father was a journeyman carpenter, one of his uncles a servant, and another a marble-cutter. His maternal grandfather had been a cobbler and his paternal grandfather a simple husbandman. Falconet's family, formerly established in the village of Exilles in the Duchy of Savoy, immigrated to Paris sometime during the seventeenth century.

Etienne's childhood, typical of a son of a Parisian artisan of modest means, was marked by down-to-earth realism. His early education was brief and elementary, and when he was still a young boy he was placed as an apprentice in the workshop of his maternal uncle, Nicolas Guillaume, who held the artisan's title of master marble-cutter. Squaring marble tops and chiseling mantelpieces until the age of eighteen, Etienne was given ample opportunity to familiarize himself with every technical process of decorative sculpture.

Very little is known about this period of Falconet's life. It is certain that in his uncle's workshop the young man came to understand a truism that is bluntly stated in de Marsy's eighteenth-century technical dictionary: "One should not confuse a *marble-cutter* with a *sculptor*." Mastering a humble craft with an assured livelihood could satisfy neither his intellectual curiosity nor his growing talent: he developed the ambition to become a true

---

[1] P.-C. Levesque, "Vie d'Etienne Falconet," in *Oeuvres complètes d'Etienne Falconet* (Paris: Dentu, 1808), I, p. 3. This "Vie" and Robin's "Eloge" (see Bibliography) are the main sources for the biographical data appearing in Chap. I.

sculptor. An inspiring example of this profession was provided by Jean-Baptiste Lemoyne, a *sculpteur du roi*, whom Etienne could have watched at work, around 1730, in his own parish church of Saint-Sauveur. Despite the active opposition of his parents and of his uncle, Falconet began to experiment surreptitiously in shaping figures in clay and wood. These artistic efforts — Falconet's youthful secretiveness was later compared to the secretiveness of Pascal at work on his early mathematical studies — became known eventually, and the apprentice marble-cutter was allowed to show his work to Jean-Baptiste Lemoyne. Impressed by the young man's talent, the famous sculptor accepted him as one of his students.

Stepping up from Nicolas Guillaume's workshop into the studio of Lemoyne (around 1734) represented an extraordinary change in Falconet's life. This studio formed some of the most esteemed sculptors of the second half of the eighteenth century, artists such as Pigalle, Pajou, Caffieri, and d'Huez: Lemoyne was universally recognized as the most successful teacher of his time. Beloved by everybody, this warm, effervescent, quasi-inarticulate little man was as much renowned for his generosity to students as he was admired for his professional skill and success. Because of the unusual length of time Falconet remained working under Lemoyne (ten years, until 1744), he achieved an exceptional place in this active studio, and a close friendship developed between the two men. The master spoke of his pupil as of his child, and Falconet affectionately acknowledged this relationship, writing toward the end of his career that he had more right to boast of having had Lemoyne as his teacher than Lemoyne had of having him as a student. Some of these feelings permeate a vigorous drawing by Lemoyne, showing the handsome, willful and concentrated face of Falconet at the age of twenty-six (Fig. 1). It is his earliest known portrait.

During his ten years with Lemoyne, Falconet underwent much more than a normal course of sculptor's training, for his professional grounding was strengthened by his participation in some of his teacher's great commissions of this period. There is little doubt, for instance, that he assisted Lemoyne in the execution of the *Basin of Neptune* group, at Versailles, and of the equestrian monument of Louis XV, at Bordeaux (Fig. 2). The experience was invaluable, but Falconet, who started his training uncommonly late, was twenty-eight years old at the time he completed his apprenticeship; that is, he was some eight years older than a typical sculptor at the same stage of his career. Furthermore, while still working under Lemoyne, he was already burdened with family responsibility: in 1739 he married Anne-Suzanne Moulin, the daughter of a cabinet-maker, and in 1741 he became the father of a son, Pierre-Etienne.

Amazingly, neither the sense of being outdistanced by younger men, nor the pressure of earning his livelihood deterred Falconet from applying his energy to another, completely different type of activity. Like the pastelist Maurice Quentin de La Tour, who yielded to the same temptation in his middle age, the sculptor decided to learn Latin when he was nearing thirty. Beginning with elementary lessons taken with a priest whom he befriended at Versailles while working for Lemoyne, Falconet achieved a most respectable degree of proficiency through strenuous application. In 1772 he published his own annotated translation of three books of Pliny the Elder's *Naturalis historia*. It is certain that the sculptor was painfully aware of the inadequacy of his early education and that, in his century, a thorough knowledge of Latin was still viewed as a more convincing proof of good upbringing than the mastery of any other subject. However, the status of Latin does not explain everything — for instance, it does not explain why Falconet, when he felt himself sufficiently strong in Latin, proceeded to learn Italian, and then started on Greek.

One senses in him a gargantuan hunger for knowledge and for intellectual self-assertion that surpasses in raw intensity all the literary ambitions of other eighteenth-century artist-writers, such as Coypel and Dandré-Bardon. In fact, Falconet's extra-professional forays into the realm of letters were not confined to linguistic *tours de force*. His avid reading brought his attention to religious questions, more particularly to Jansenism and to Protestantism, and then to philosophy. In philosophy, as in religion, he seems to have been searching for a certain element of rigoristic purity. He failed to find it in the writings of eighteenth-century philosophers. Returning to classical authors, he read Diogenes Laërtius' biography of Greek philosophers and Plato in the Dacier translation; as a result, he developed a sort of cult for the figure of Socrates, whom he singled out as a model. He felt a direct affinity for the great philosopher who, according to tradition, had first been trained as a sculptor, and he was fascinated by the physical resemblance he saw between himself and the features recorded in the busts of Plato's teacher.

Falconet's admiration for Socrates is a curious psychological phenomenon that evidently transcends a purely intellectual interest in philosophy. This admiration went so far as to lead him to pseudo-Socratic mimicry: he adopted the plainest clothes, his mode of life was marked by uncommon frugality, and he maintained this exaggerated austerity even much later in life, at a time of comparative prosperity. In accordance with the same Socratic image, the sculptor was prone to irony, and in his conversations, he took delight in entrapping his antagonists into systematic *ad absurdum* arguments. Predictably, most of Falconet's contemporaries associated such an attitude with eccentricity, pretentious affectation, gruffness, and sarcasm. Yet they did not fail to sense a powerful personality. Diderot observed that since the qualities and the flaws of Falconet's character paralleled, to a degree, those of Jean-Jacques Rousseau, the artist was appropriately nicknamed "the Jean-Jacques of sculpture."

At the time he was concluding his apprenticeship under Lemoyne, Falconet had to face the question of his future as an independent sculptor. His growing erudition and his philosophical interests had not brought him closer to the traditional point of departure for such a future: acceptance in the Royal Academy — the *Académie royale de peinture et de sculpture*.

The problem was a weighty one, for no artist seriously concerned with his career could afford to ignore indefinitely this official body. The Royal Academy had been founded in 1648 for the purpose of asserting the ennobling aspect of the artist's profession, contrasting the status of artist to that of artisan of the guild. During the eighteenth century the Academy had become the supreme organization of the arts in France, commanding great power and prestige. It defended the interests and the privileges of its members, it assumed responsibility for the education of gifted young artists, and it established the standards of professional accomplishment. In addition, most significantly, the Academy enjoyed total monopoly of the Salon exhibitions that insured official "visibility" to their participants. Although placed under the protection of the king, the Academy was allowed a good measure of independence from royal agencies, and its essential day-to-day business was transacted through deliberations, vote, and elected committees.

The artists of the Academy were organized into a rather rigid hierarchy, and acceptance of a new member was by no means to be taken for granted. Falconet did not encounter great difficulty with the lowest rung of the ladder, when at the age of twenty-eight he decided to make his move: he was voted in as *agréé*, that is, approved aspirant, on his first try, upon the submission of his terra-cotta model of *Milo of Crotona* (August 29, 1744). The humble rank of *agréé* represented no more than a preliminary stamp of approval, but this first success gave Falconet the privilege of exhibiting in the official Salon alongside the most celebrated artists. There was a proviso: the new privilege was not a permanent right unless the *agréé* became a full-fledged academician. In other words, this privilege could be annulled if the sculptor failed to complete his *morceau de réception*, the required reception piece, to the satisfaction of the Academy. For Falconet, unexpected complications arose. Usually the *morceau de réception* was the marble rendition of the plaster model originally submitted by the candidate to become an *agréé*. However, the Academy's jury decided that Falconet's *Milo of Crotona* could not be accepted as a model for his *morceau de réception* because it recalled too closely the *Milo* of the great seventeenth-century sculptor Pierre Puget.

Thus, one month after Falconet was accepted as an *agréé*, the Director of the Academy assigned him a completely new subject for his *morceau de réception*: the *Allegory of Sculpture*. In addition, in order to prevent any possibility of outside help, the sculptor was required to execute this work in a studio of the *vieux Louvre*, on the premises of the Academy. While "legal" according to Academy rules, these mortifying conditions were seldom fully imposed. The allegation of plagiarism, clearly unjustified, and the consequent unpleasant rulings strongly suggest that the abrasive ways of the Jean-Jacques of sculpture aroused very early active antagonism in the Academy.

Falconet had no alternative but to comply. A year later, he submitted a terra-cotta sketch of the *Allegory of Sculpture* (1745), followed by a full-scale terra-cotta model (1746) that received the approval of the Academy. A last step still remained. In order to satisfy all the requirements for his investiture as a full academician, he was expected to execute, within another year, the final marble rendition of the same *Allegory*. It is difficult to conjecture about what happened at this point. After a long series of extensions granted to the sculptor to complete his work (it was eventually completed, at an undetermined date), the Academy unexpectedly reversed itself; on August 31, 1754, Falconet was received as academician — not upon the presentation of the *Allegory of Sculpture* but on that of the marble version of his old *Milo of Crotona*. The statue had apparently ceased to recall Puget in the eyes of the judges. Exactly ten years had lapsed between Falconet's acceptance as *agréé* and his becoming a full academician.

After this, Falconet's academic progress continued at a more normal pace. He was elected *adjoint à professeur*, roughly equivalent to assistant professor, in 1755, less than a year after his appointment as an academician. With this rank, he joined the influential teaching staff of the Academy and entered the mainstream of the Academy's multiple activities. He partook regularly in the deliberations of the institution, he served several times on its budget and its exhibition committees, and he drew up the regulations designed to uphold order and decency in life-classes (a perennial problem among students). Most notably, he was granted the honor of reading an essay to the assembly, *Réflexions sur la sculpture* (June 7, 1760), which was later published as an article in Diderot's famous *Encyclopedia*.

Falconet inspired more respect than affection. His attitude toward students was often marked by harshness and his conversation with them studded with diatribes. During a students' competition, he openly humiliated his son, Pierre-Etienne, a would-be painter, in front of his fellow academicians, and in a surge of Socratic stoicism, took it upon himself to remove his offspring's mediocre entry from the contestants' exhibition. Another time, Falconet publicly offended one of his former students, Nicolas Sénéchal, in the presence of the latter's family, reportedly causing the desperate young man to drown himself in a well. One must keep in mind, however, that Falconet's humiliation of his son is reported by Diderot to illustrate the "Roman" streak in the sculptor's character, while the alleged suicide of Sénéchal is introduced by Robespierre's friend, the painter Jacques-Louis David, in a vicious harangue he delivered during the Revolution to expose the injustices of the Royal Academy. Yet such anecdotes recur throughout Falconet's career, and despite probable exaggerations, they seem to underline a definite trend in his behavior.

Rather than gratuitous sadism, these incidents suggest extreme self-righteousness, self-will, and easily provoked irascibility. The sculptor was quite capable of generosity to his students. Shortly before submitting his *morceau de réception*, he successfully interceded in favor of one of his students, Félix Lecomte, who had been expelled from the Academy's school for having threatened to destroy the still-unfinished marble group of *Milo of Crotona* (1752). This was great magnanimity in view of the fact that the group was precisely the final *morceau de réception* Falconet was preparing for his election as an academician.

Armed with Socratic wit whetted by choleric disposition, the sculptor could be a formidable adversary or a most useful ally. The young Joseph-Marie Vien, who was to become the father of French Neoclassic painting, found in Falconet a providential champion. The sculptor saved the painter from rejection as an *agréé* by effectively ridiculing the old-fashioned bias of the academic judges who were reluctant to tolerate a style different from their own.

All in all, in spite of his peculiarities, Falconet had only one overt enemy among his colleagues in the Academy: Jean-Baptiste Pigalle, the celebrated sculptor of the *Mercury Fastening His Heel-Wings*. Doubtless, jealousy played a part in Falconet's feelings. Pigalle, although only two years older, had won his academic seniority far more rapidly and had succeeded in attracting a far greater number of important commissions. Falconet's contemporaries thought that this jealousy was the reason for his unfortunate involvement in the notorious Bouchardon-Pigalle-Vassé affair. Before his death (1762) Edmé Bouchardon chose Pigalle to complete his unfinished, but already much admired, equestrian statue of Louis XV. Louis-Claude Vassé, however was tempted by the importance of the under-taking; encouraged by the Comte de Caylus, who felt that Pigalle's art lacked the necessary classical quality, Vassé tried to take the commission away from Pigalle by claiming that he could execute the work for half the price. Falconet, apparently hoping to discredit Pigalle by exposing his greed, lent himself to the scheme and wrote an "expert's certificate" to justify the reasonableness of Vassé's contention.

This murky episode gained too much notoriety to be left unmentioned here, but Falconet should not be too hastily cast in the role of a man sacrificing his integrity to his enmity. The true meaning of his action is hopelessly blurred in the confusion of rivalry, intrigue, and calumny that plagued the academic milieu. The character of Falconet's animosity is perhaps more fairly expressed in a statement he made on the occasion of the unveiling of Pigalle's own monument of Louis XV, commissioned for the city of Rheims (1763):

> Monsieur Pigalle, I do not like you and I believe that you feel the same about me. I have seen your *Citizen* [one of the figures of Pigalle's monument]; it is possible to make something as beautiful as this figure, since you did it; but I do not think that art could rise a hairbreadth above. This will not prevent our relationship from remaining as it was.[2]

One can understand that Falconet could hardly have become a popular figure. On the other hand, he had several good friends in the Academy, and it would be a mistake to think that he was an atrabilious solitary. Besides Lemoyne, who liked to call Falconet his child, one finds among his friends and direct collaborators two of the most influential artists of the Academy: François Boucher, the favorite painter of Madame de Pompadour, and Jean-Baptiste-Marie Pierre, the first painter to the Duc d'Orléans. Ironically, it is probable that Boucher liked Falconet because he identified the sculptor's studied simplicity with his own, very genuine, commonness, while the pretentious and well-educated Pierre was drawn to Falconet because he recognized in him a kindred spirit, the humanistically oriented artist-litterateur.

Outside his academic occupations, Falconet's professional activity was unavoidably bound to the existing system of patronage and commissions. Their most obvious source was the King of France, or more precisely, his Directeur des Bâtiments, whose functions corresponded to those of a minister of fine arts. In Falconet's time, this position was held by Le Normant de Tournehem, until 1751, and from then on by the Marquise de Pompadour's brother, the Marquis de Marigny. Of several commissions Falconet received through this official sponsorship, only one, *France Embracing the Bust of Louis XV*, was actually intended for the monarch. Most of the others were executed for Madame de Pompadour, the king's favorite. Many of these works — the most important of them were *The Allegory of Music* and *The Menacing Cupid* — were part of the decoration of her châteaux and places of residence, such as Bellevue, Crécy, Saint-Hubert, Choisy, and the Hôtel d'Evreux.

There is no evidence that the Marquise de Pompadour had ever spoken to Falconet:

[2] Reported in Diderot's *Salon of 1765*. Diderot, *Oeuvres complètes*, ed. by J. Assézat and M. Tourneux (Paris: Garnier, 1876), X, p. 427.

like many of her sculptors, he remained in the shadow of Boucher, who had a far greater opportunity to approach their illustrious patron. Falconet had mixed feelings about the Marquise. He writes ironically of her love for the arts "which she had neither the time nor the talent to cultivate"; yet, gratefully acknowledging her help to the artists, he adds that "she paid well, and one worked well for her."[3] In fact, the sculptor did much more for Madame de Pompadour than contribute to the splendor of her surroundings. In 1757 he was appointed director of the sculpture studios of the royal manufacture of ceramics of Sèvres; in this position he was entrusted with the implementation of one of the Marquise's most cherished ideas for a national French art. Madame de Pompadour, patriot in her own way, was the guiding spirit of the ceramic enterprise that was intended to challenge the European monopoly of Meissen with the creation of the *porcelaine de France*. Once a week, for almost ten years (from 1757 to 1766, at a salary of 2400 *livres* a year), Falconet rode from Paris to Sèvres to bring new models and to supervise the operation of the *Atelier de Sculpture*. Although concerned with the production of small white porcelain statuettes, called *biscuits*, Falconet's activity at Sèvres came to assume a definite historical significance in terms of eighteenth-century stylistic diffusion. Because of a new technique of very precise reproduction of three-dimensional forms in ceramic, sculptural models created by Falconet for Sèvres could be multiplied by means of these biscuits, as many times and almost as faithfully, as two-dimensional designs could be multiplied through a printing process.

Madame de Pompadour's patronage attracted a few commissions from the circle of higher nobility. One of her closest friends, the Prince de Soubise, ordered from Falconet reliefs of the *Four Seasons*, and the ruler of Württemberg, the Duke Charles Eugene, asked him to execute allegories of the *Sovereignty of Princes* and the *Glory of Princes* for his palace of Stuttgart. Yet most of Falconet's patrons were financiers and magistrates belonging to the wealthy but less exalted *noblesse de robe*. Thus members of a family of parliamentarians, the Thiroux, became the owners of the *Bather* and of the *Pygmalion and Galatea*. In the same social group, the family of the attorney-general, Guillaume-François Joly de Fleury, commissioned his funeral monument in the church of Saint-André-des-Arts. Among the *noblesse de robe*, Falconet's most important patron was undoubtedly Ange-Laurent de La Live de Jully, the wealthy son of a *fermier général* (collector of revenues). Besides being the brother-in-law of Madame d'Epinay (the benefactress of Jean-Jacques Rousseau) and the brother of Madame d'Houdetot (one of Rousseau's passions), La Live de Jully was a gifted amateur artist and one of the great art collectors of his century. His *Cabinet français* — exclusively devoted to French art — included no less than three examples of Falconet's work. His interest in the sculptor was also evidenced by two original commissions: the statue of *Sweet Melancholy* and the design of his first wife's tomb, in the church of Saint-Roch. Significantly, Falconet was chosen as one of the delegates sent to La Live de Jully to express the Academy's gratitude for his gift of Le Brun's painting, *The Death of Cato of Utica*.

[3] Falconet, *Oeuvres diverses concernant les arts* (Paris: Didot and Jombert, 1787), I, p. 231. This edition of Falconet's *Oeuvres*, the last edition published during his lifetime, has been used as the basic source for Falconet's writings quoted or referred to in this book.

Ecclesiastical art was not as alien to Voltaire's century as it is commonly believed, and the most elaborate single project entrusted to Falconet before his gigantic monument of Peter the Great was the redecoration of the Parisian church of Saint-Roch under the guidance of the *curé* Marduel. The project, which was stretched over seven years (1753-1760), brought the sculptor a very disappointing financial reward — which he describes in a letter written to the Marquis de Marigny (June 4, 1765) as "bread and masses."

Considering the matter of financial reward, it seems strange that Falconet apparently nursed an almost morbid aversion toward bust portraiture — the most reliable potboiler of his profession from time immemorial. Relinquishing most of the bust commissions to his pupil, Marie-Anne Collot, he left only four known sculpted portraits.

The income he could derive from his other commissions was anything but predictable. Without his royal pension (which eventually amounted to a yearly maximum of 1000 *livres*) and the annual stipend of 2400 *livres* he was receiving for his work at Sèvres (with an additional percentage on the sale of biscuits), the sculptor could not have been assured a stable livelihood. It is certain that his beginnings had taught him a lasting lesson. This explains why Falconet, in spite of his many occupations, still found time and energy to supply decorative designs for some luxury crafts. In this category were the models of the two candlesticks ordered by the great silversmith Germain, exhibited in the Salon of 1761. These candlesticks were the only example of the sculptor's work in the "minor arts" ever shown in the Salon. Similarly, with the exception of the *Little Girl Hiding Cupid's Bow*, also displayed in the Salon of 1761, he never chose to exhibit his models for the Sèvres biscuits.

Falconet's attitude is understandable. However lucrative, such commercially conceived undertakings unavoidably added to the bitterness of a man who liked to give an appearance of loftiness and austerity. A suggestion of watered ideals and an artisan-like attitude would doubtless have been especially irritating at the time of the sculptor's deepening involvement in the prestigious world of letters.

This involvement becomes conspicuous around 1760. In 1759, after years of lukewarm praise, at the very moment his *Menacing Cupid* and his *Bather* were beginning to stimulate some enthusiasm in the Salon, Falconet's work at Saint-Roch was subjected to a concerted assault. The experience proved to be most useful. Inept barbs, directed at the "lack of illusion" of the marble clouds of the *Glory* of Saint-Roch, did not do great damage to the artist's reputation. However, while fighting nonentities like Madame de Pompadour's librarian, Philippe Bridard de la Garde, Falconet gained an influential ally: Charles-Nicolas Cochin. This famous engraver and writer most opportunely introduced the ludicrous quarrel of Saint-Roch in *Les Misotechnites aux enfers* (1763), one of the eighteenth-century's wittiest satires on critics.

Under the pretext of exposing the inaneness of Falconet's detractors, this little book cast a strong light on a problem that will have explosive cultural consequences in the following century: the confrontation between the critic and the artist. Eighteenth-century critics, for the most part recruited from the ranks of the literati, held that since everyone had accepted the sisterhood of art and literature, following Horace, there was no reason why art should be spared the attacks that so indiscriminatingly befell literature. The artists, who were often inarticulate and defenseless against such attacks, kept repeating that men of letters should be disqualified as critics, since only those who actually practiced an art were competent to talk about it. Such statements and counterstatements furthered the coalescence of two images: the man of letters in the role of the incompetent but professional art critic, and the artist in the role of the occasional writer, somewhat awkward, but fully informed and burning with vengeance.

In his discussion of the Saint-Roch episode, Cochin proclaimed that not only was Falconet's critic de la Garde utterly incompetent to judge art, but also that he was less competent *as a man of letters* than the sculptor. Coming from Cochin, who was anything but awkward as a writer and who enjoyed a well-established literary authority, such a contention suggests that Falconet had already won a reputation as an articulate writer.

In building this reputation, the sculptor had been seconded by one of the leading philosophers of the century: Denis Diderot. In 1760, Falconet was asked to write an article on sculpture for Diderot's *Encyclopedia* (as already noted, the article was published after having been read at one of the sessions of the Academy). Such a request from Denis Diderot was indeed flattering. It was proudly acknowledged as a mark of approval by the sculptor, who guided the famous philosopher through Salon exhibitions and came to act as his technical art consultant. By 1765 they had become close friends. They often spent long hours together by the fireside in Diderot's study, rue Taranne, discussing art and philosophy. In their conversations, on such topics as art criticism, the social status of the artist, the role of Antiquity, and the necessity of creative freedom, they often came back to a theme that captivated both of them: the judgment of posterity as a stimulant for the creative man. Diderot had faith in its importance, while Falconet discounted it, maintaining that he was interested only in the acclaim of his own time.

These discussions, growing in subtlety, were eventually pursued in the form of a long exchange of letters, which the two friends agreed to publish. Diderot treated Falconet — essentially an autodidact — as his intellectual equal. Referring to this correspondence, which he was polishing for publication, Diderot wrote to his friend Sophie Volland: "You will see me in these letters as a very estimable madman, and Falconet as a very vain and very subtle sophist."[4]

For Diderot, however, Falconet was also fascinating as the embodiment of a certain type of creative man whose makeup was a pattern of contradictions — a concept he had already developed, on a fictional plane, in the oddities of his *Neveu de Rameau*. This is clearly shown in the lengthy portrait of Falconet that appears in Diderot's *Salon of 1765*:

> Here is a man who is endowed with genius, and who has all kinds of qualities compatible and incompatible with genius . . . for he has plenty of finesse, taste, wit, tact, sweetness, and grace; for he is boorish and polite, affable and abrupt, tender and hard; for he models clay and marble, and he reads and meditates; for he is gentle and caustic, serious and gay; for he is a philosopher, he believes in nothing, and well knows why; for he is a good father, and his son ran away from home; for he was madly in love with his mistress, and he made her suffer to death, and, for that reason, he became sad, somber, melancholy, he thought he would die of remorse,

---

[4] Diderot, *Lettres à Sophie Volland*, ed. by A. Babelon (Paris: Gallimard, 1930), III, p. 272.

and he lost her long ago, and he has not yet consoled himself. To this, you can add that there is no man more eager for the approval of his contemporaries and more indifferent to that of posterity. He carries this philosophy to an incredible point, and he told me a hundred times that he would not give an *écu* to insure the immortality of the most beautiful of his statues.[5]

This many-faceted characterization of Falconet at the age of forty-nine does not reveal a very happy man. A number of additional acid touches could be added to this portrait. The recent Bouchardon-Pigalle-Vassé scandal had cast an unpleasant shadow on the sculptor's professional integrity. Moreover, his academic career and the extent of royal recognition had been somewhat disappointing. He had been a full professor since 1761, but his pension was considerably smaller than that of academicians with comparable seniority. He had lost his right to the customary studio in the Louvre, and his talent was never acknowledged by royal honors, such as the Order of Saint-Michel, which was bestowed on many of his colleagues. Finally, after the death in 1764 of his most trustworthy patron, Madame de Pompadour, his economic future was becoming uncertain. His life seemed marked by unfulfilled hopes, and despite the success of his *Pygmalion* (1763) — a success which, in his view, was very far from the triumph of Pigalle's monument to Louis XV — he felt that he had not yet achieved any work deserving recognition.

Considering this state of mind, one can imagine Falconet's exhilaration upon receiving the invitation to come to Russia to execute the monument to Peter the Great.

Initially, several other French sculptors had been approached by the Russians, and the negotiations were proceeding at a slow pace. Diderot's friendship with Prince Galitzine, the Russian ambassador at the court of Versailles, was instrumental in mustering most of the political influence for granting the commission to Falconet. But the sculptor's self-restraint provided the decisive argument. Among those competing for the same work, Pajou requested 600,000 *livres*, Saly, 480,000, Coustou, 450,000, and Vassé, 400,000. Remembering the unpleasantness of the Bouchardon-Pigalle-Vassé affair, and retroactively proving his integrity at his own expense, Falconet refused the offer of 300,000 *livres*, insisting the payment be limited to only 200,000.

Accompanied by his eighteen-year old pupil, Marie-Anne Collot, who was probably already his mistress, Falconet left for Russia on September 12, 1766. Two assistant workmen and a molder were supposed to join them later in Saint Petersburg. The heavy baggage had been sent by sea from Rouen. It consisted of twenty-five large bundles filled with casts, books, prints, and paintings. Among other things, this shipment contained Boucher's *Pygmalion and Galatea* (a gift from the Royal Academy to the Academy of Saint Petersburg), Mademoiselle Collot's busts of Diderot and of Prince Galitzine, and models of most of Falconet's statuary. It also included three unfinished works by Falconet that were to be purchased from their original patrons by the Russian Empress: the *Sovereignty* and the *Glory of Princes* (formerly destined for the Duke of Württemberg), and the figure of *Winter* (originally commissioned by Madame de Pompadour).

Falconet had prepared himself for a long and productive sojourn. In fact, he remained in Russia from 1766 to 1778, four years longer than the eight years anticipated in the leave of absence granted him before his departure by the Marquis de Marigny. Catherine II

[5] Diderot, *Oeuvres complètes*, X, p. 426.

welcomed the artist at her court of Saint Petersburg with open arms. For her, he was more than a sculptor — he was the first representative of the prestigious literary circles of Paris to appear in Russia. She considered Falconet as a direct messenger of the French *philosophes*, for whom she professed unbounded admiration, and she called him: "*l'ami de l'âme de Diderot*" — "the friend of the soul of Diderot." Although differently motivated, the sculptor was equally enthusiastic. He had never before had the opportunity of coming so close to a monarch. Despite his self-assertion as a commoner, he could not avoid being dazzled by the Empress's graciousness and by the feeling of intellectual fellowship she insisted on preserving in their letters.

For the first time in his career, he could taste honors and adulation. He was immediately accepted as a "free honorary associate" in the Academy of Saint Petersburg; he was subjected to courtiers' flattery; and he was plagued by requests for recommendation to the Empress, which were coming from Russians as well as from fellow Frenchmen who had not paid great attention to him in Paris. His living quarters were conveniently situated near the Winter Palace, and Carburi-Laskary, the Greek engineer in the service of Catherine II, built him a huge studio, of a new and daring design. Everything was ready for the great enterprise of Peter the Great's statue. Falconet eagerly immersed himself in his work: for the first time in his life circumstances allowed him to give full measure to his talent as a sculptor. This atmosphere of active and victorious anticipation is echoed in a bust executed about this time (1768) by Mademoiselle Collot (Fig. 3). The young sculptress gave her beloved teacher the look of a gentle, unassuming, witty philosopher — one thinks of a character from Greuze posing as Voltaire. However, behind this eighteenth-century mixture of sensibility and irony, the slightly weathered face of the Jean-Jacques of sculpture radiates with a still-youthful energy, self-confidence, and joy.

In Saint Petersburg, intrigue was no less rampant than in Paris. Trusting a clause of his contract stating that he was subject to the orders of the Empress only, Falconet took little account of the existing configuration of power and influence at the court. Thus he made the serious mistake of bypassing old General Betzki, Catherine's pet gossip as well as her minister of fine arts. Enraged by Falconet's indifference to his opinions, the sly octogenarian, who had planned to use the sculptor as mere executant for his own conception of the monument, devoted a great deal of energy to harassing the sculptor and to discrediting him in the eyes of the Empress.

This persecution coincided with problems in the artist's own household. Diderot arrived in Russia in 1773, eagerly looking forward to a reunion with his friend, but he was informed, to his dismay, that there was no room for him in the sculptor's house. This astonishing lack of hospitality, which broke their friendship, was related to the visit of Falconet's son, Pierre-Etienne, now a mediocre painter, who had come to Saint Petersburg from England in the hope of exploiting his father's success. It would appear that at the time of Diderot's visit, the sculptor was undergoing a serious personal crisis in his relations with Mademoiselle Collot. Pierre-Etienne was the cause: in 1775 Falconet's mistress and Falconet's son made a joint voyage to France, and in 1777 they were married in Saint Petersburg.

The sculptor's growing unhappiness was also rooted in other factors. At the beginning, his work proceeded rapidly, and the great plaster model of the statue was publicly exhibited in 1770. But from then on, despite Catherine's praise, progress slackened to a discouraging snail's pace. The major problem was the casting of the gigantic statue in bronze. This difficult operation was hindered by a succession of wasteful delays caused by a variety of technical accidents and the inefficiency of the workmen. In terms of drama and frustration, the casting of *Peter the Great* surpassed the saga of Benvenuto Cellini's colossal *Mars*. By 1774, Falconet's patience was exhausted; he decided to discharge his head founder and to assume himself the direction of the operation (according to his contract, he was not responsible for this phase of the execution). Finally, after a partial failure in 1775, the work was successfully completed in 1777.

By that time, Betzki, who had done his best to disseminate his belittling interpretation of Falconet's predicaments, succeeded in securing his disgrace. Overwhelmed with humiliation at a time he should have been enjoying triumph, the disheartened artist left Saint Petersburg in September 1778, four years before the official inauguration of his statue.

Falconet compared his westbound crossing of the Russian border to an escape from prison: "I felt my chest expanding and my blood, more fluid, circulating with a smooth- ness which I have almost ceased to experience."[6] Instead of going directly to Paris, he went first to The Hague, where he was invited to stay at the home of Prince Galitzine. He remained two years in the Netherlands. The greater part of this time was spent in the preparation of the first complete edition of his written work, most of which had been composed in Russia during the long periods of imposed idleness (*Observations on the Statue of Marcus Aurelius, Translation of Pliny*, etc.).

Taking great pride in his connoisseurship, Falconet was settling down in the role of an enlightened litterateur. His sculpting days were over. He behaved as an onlooker, an art critic, expressing his carefully termed admiration for the group portraits of Van der Helst in Amsterdam, discussing the naturalism of Rubens's *Descent from the Cross* in Antwerp, and indignantly correcting a false Rubens attribution of a Van Dyck in Brussels.

Back in Paris, in November 1780, he requested that the Academy excuse him from active teaching and place him on the retired list. Yet, thrust into fame by the growing reputation of *Peter the Great*, he accepted his appointment in 1783 to the important adminis- trative position of Assistant Rector of the Academy. He was given little time to savor these honors. The same year, two days before starting on an Italian trip — a long postponed dream — he suffered a stroke that paralyzed the right half of his body. He spent his last eight years in his apartment in the rue Regratière, on the Ile Saint-Louis, a perversely cranky invalid, devotedly nursed by his daughter-in-law (her unhappy marriage to Falconet's son had ended in a sordid scandal). His intellect and his willpower were intact, and he had sufficient energy to learn to write and to draw with his left hand. He died on January 24, 1791, and was buried in the church of Saint-Louis-en-l'Ile. Occurring at a time of mounting Revolutionary upheavals, his death did not attract great attention. Thus the following year Catherine II wrote to the Baron von Grimm that she had been

---

[6] Falconet, *Oeuvres diverses*, III, p. 378.

so provoked by the victory of the French Revolutionary army at Valmy that she could hardly pay any notice to the death of Falconet.

The sculptor did not die in poverty. His estate, which included an extensive library as well as a collection of paintings, drawings, and prints, was valued at the considerable sum of 263,000 *livres*. It was divided between his son and his daughter-in-law. Pierre-Etienne died only five months after his father, while Marie-Anne Collot lived until 1821. Their daughter, Marie-Lucie, born during their sojourn in Saint Petersburg, married the Baron de Jankowitz, a Polish nobleman established in Lorraine. Her death, in 1866, marks the end of the direct line of Falconet's descendants.

II

Acceptance in the Academy
and the Search for a Style

ABSOLUTELY nothing is known of Falconet's independent sculptural accomplishments before 1744, the date of his acceptance as an *agréé*. Thus, a study of his artistic "starting point" may usefully begin with the two statues he conceived for the Academy around that time: the *Milo of Crotona* and the *Allegory of Sculpture*.

Falconet's work on the *Milo of Crotona* was spread over ten years, from the terra-cotta model of 1744 to the final marble rendition of 1754, now in the Louvre (Fig. 6). The subject was the story of a Greek athlete of the sixth century B.C., famous for his extraordinary feats of strength. He was the Samson of the Classical age. One day, the aging Milo, wishing to put his declining muscular power to the test, tried to tear apart a tree trunk that had been partially split by woodcutters. The tree closed on his hand, and the athlete died a defenseless prisoner, devoured by the wild beasts of the forest. Popularized by authors of mythologies, who repeated Classical writers like Valerius Maximus, the legend inspired a number of paintings, engravings, and statues prior to Falconet.

In order to visualize the *Milo* of Falconet in the perspective of the eighteenth century, it may be useful to summarize Diderot's comprehensive discussion of the statue, which appears in a letter written to Prince Galitzine. The following is a paraphrase of Diderot's comments:

> Falconet did not think of placing himself in the predicament of his hero. Milo seems to be doing more shouting than fighting, and he should have used his left arm and his left foot to strike at the lion, instead of letting himself be "eaten like a fool." The figure is of a most common, vulgar type. In contrast with the noble agony of the famous Classical group of the *Laocoon* (Fig. 4), Milo's grimacing suffering has neither dignity nor elevation, and it makes one think of an accomplice of the bandit Cartouche, dying on the wheel. Moreover, Milo's anatomy is bizarre: the abdomen shows uncomprehensible folds of flesh and cavities, the left arm is twisted, and the right foot is distorted by exostosis. The tensions of the various parts of

the body are not in harmony, and the figure lacks inner unity of action. Thus, the lower portion of Milo's figure — lifted from the *Laocoön* — conveys indeed a feeling of suffering, but this feeling disappears in the upper part, and the right arm, caught in the tree, is paradoxically free from any suggestion of pain. As for Falconet's design: the execution of the figure lacks fullness, and the marble surface is marked by knobs which cause the eyes to blink. In his eagerness to show Milo's body in its entirety, the sculptor, forgetting that there could not exist any real beauty without truth, resorted to a contrived arrangement of his subject.

Despite its glaring animosity — Diderot's letter was written in 1774, immediately after his break with Falconet — this analysis is a revealing example of the type of reasoning to be expected from a well-informed eighteenth-century critic. Beyond any doubt, such reasoning was quite familiar to the sculptor at the time he was preparing his group for the Academy, and the same kind of literary rationalization was used by most of the other critics to praise the *Milo* when it appeared in the Salon.

To be accepted as an *agréé* or to become a full academician, Falconet was expected to demonstrate his technical competence in his *morceau de réception*, insofar as it could be judged from factors like the perfection of his carving, his anatomical science, and his knowledge of compositional rules. But, more importantly, he was also expected to display his inventiveness and to show his ability to exploit the potential expressiveness of his subject. In the eighteenth-century artistic vocabulary, the term "expression" alludes, above all, to the rendition of the various states of the soul, such as anger, love, and horror. In a work of art, these states of the soul, or "passions," were defined by the character of the hero, his age, his social position, and by the particular circumstances that caused their stimulation.

In this light, most of Diderot's remarks can plausibly be applied to Falconet's *Milo*. But today, of course, one cannot seriously confine oneself to this standard of criticism. One does not mind in the least the alleged absence of Milo's nobility, and one no longer dares to consider tragic occurrences in Diderot's analytical manner. Moreover, photography demonstrates that episodes of great violence and emotional upheaval can assume unpredictable form. It is also possible to produce countless examples of twentieth-century art to prove that emotions of great intensity can be successfully conveyed without the benefit of logic or recognizable representation. Since everything in Falconet's *Milo* may appear plausible to the modern eye, Diderot's criticism is too narrowly rational to be convincing.

One of Diderot's comments provides a stepping-stone to a specialized modern approach. Diderot blamed the sculptor for not having imagined himself in Milo's place. Curiously, this criticism is refuted by Falconet himself. He is reported to have said that Milo's head was "without nobility" because he did it after his own head — and allowing for the obvious difference of expression, one may note that the head of Milo (Fig. 7), with its broad face and its upturned nose, is reminiscent of Falconet's features in Lemoyne's drawing of 1741 (Fig. 1). Thus, in all probability, the sculptor did indeed imagine himself in the predicament of his pathetic hero. This self-identification opens a vista crisscrossed with inviting Freudian and Jungian paths. Naturally many artists — for instance, Dürer, Raphael, and Rembrandt — represented themselves in their works. Such representations, introduced for a variety of reasons (religious symbolism, social standing, added sense of immediacy, etc.), belong to the stock-in-trade of the art profession and should not be too readily reinterpreted in the perspective of another age. Yet, without placing Falconet posthumously on a couch, one must acknowledge that the *Milo of Crotona* was his first important work and that it was executed during a period of personal hardship and unusually trying professional pressures. It is not too farfetched to surmise that the sculptor found in the theme of Milo of Crotona a symbolical expression of his own anxiety.

Whatever the *Milo's* hidden autobiographical meaning, an objective stylistic study shows that the statue has the earmarks of an early work, with a good measure of discernable derivations from earlier art. A glance at the famous seventeenth-century *Milo* of Puget (Fig. 5) is sufficient to prove that despite the Academic judges' criticism, the heroically massive, standing statue could not have been one of Falconet's sources. In fact, the small size of Falconet's work (about $27\frac{1}{4}$ inches), the position of the hero, thrown on his back, and the fastidiously detailed staging are quite characteristic of an eighteenth-century *morceau de réception*. Not surprisingly, the indented silhouette of Falconet's group echoes the capricious playfulness of Rococo ornamentation, and the Rococo spirit is also felt in the rhythmic ripples that outline some of the forms (Fig. 8). But if Falconet unavoidably captured something of the prevailing stylistic mode of his century, it is apparent that he followed several other directions, involving both Classical and Baroque elements.

The influence of the *Laocoön*, already noted by Diderot, is not the only instance of Falconet's inspiration by late Classical art — the entire attitude of Milo's faun-like figure parallels a type that occurs in a number of Hellenistic and Roman friezes. And Italian Baroque sculpture, greatly admired in Falconet's writings, is not forgotten: playing the part of Milo, the sculptor gave to his own face the theatrically grimacing expression of horror of Bernini's *Damned Soul* (Rome, Palazzo di Spagna) (another opening for a speculative analysis of Falconet's personality!). The Baroque quality is also reflected in bits of naturalistic emphasis, such as the tuft of hair on Milo's chest, the convincing texturing of the tree stump and of the lion's mane, and the heavy, blanket-like, decoratively whirling drapery. Above all, the influence of Bernini, and the general influence of Baroque art — possibly involving one of Rubens's lion hunts — is expressed in the almost sadistic immediacy of the drama and in the diagonal movements recurring throughout the composition.

It would be a mistake, however, to consider the *Milo of Crotona* as a mere mosaic of "visual quotations." Borrowings are focused by Falconet's vision and fused into the impetuosity of his staging. Like the young Rembrandt in the *Blinding of Samson* (Frankfurt, Staedel Institute), the young Falconet is overplaying and overacting to the hilt, and because of these very overstatements, his group conveys a feeling of naïve sincerity as well as bravura. Through the sculptor's eclecticism, one begins to detect the emergence of personal artistic qualities. Thus, regardless of questions of derivation, Milo's acrobatic posture reveals a very personal feeling for resilient anatomical elegance. Similarly, despite the Rococo format and the Baroque inspiration, the systematic opposition and the mutual neutralization of diagonal movements bring about a most un-Bernniesque compositional self-containment.

All in all, the work of Falconet appears as an appealingly awkward, deliberate attempt to bring vivifying naturalism and pathos into the formula of a Rococo *morceau de réception* and to revaluate the vocabulary of Bernini in terms of a tightly knit compositional logic. Both trends will become essential to French art. Admittedly, Falconet did not yet succeed in bringing these trends into a harmonic equilibrium, and his Milo makes one think of a Hellenistic or a Baroque faun caught in the rigorous geometry of a Classical metope.

The *Allegory of Sculpture* (Fig. 9) was a far less demanding theme than the *Milo of Crotona*, but it would have been difficult to find a less inspiring one. Holding a chisel and leaning on the antique *Belvedere Torso*, the subject of personified Sculpture imposed on Falconet belonged to the category of allegorical clichés that has been monotonously repeated through centuries.

It is probable that the total lack of interest evoked by this commonplace emblematic theme influenced the judgment of the few critics who paid any attention to the statue. Thus, speaking of Falconet's full-scale terra-cotta model of this *Allegory*, exhibited in the Salon of 1746, the prominent critic Lafont de Saint-Yenne succinctly praised the correctness and the knowledge of the sculptor, observed the insipidity and the lack of character of the statue, and concluded by reporting that visitors to the Salon did not find the idea of the allegory had been fulfilled by the composition. Writing on Falconet two centuries later, Louis Réau displayed even less interest than his eighteenth-century predecessor and described the *Allegory* as an ill-born production that was imposed on the artist and that was executed under the worst conditions.

This mood of disappointment can be easily dispelled by a visit to the Victoria and Albert Museum. If one can forget the uninteresting subject matter and the frustrating circumstances surrounding the conception of the statue, the final (undated) marble version of the *Allegory of Sculpture* (Fig. 9) emerges, in spite of its small size (about $25\frac{1}{4}$ inches), as one of the most impressive of Falconet's early productions.

The carving is far more complex than that of the *Milo*. Falconet's new treatment of the marble surface becomes apparent in the figure's drapery, which, for evident reasons, is given far greater care than that of his earlier statue. The changing pattern of the folds suggests two different fabrics: a heavy, blanket-like drapery — reminiscent of that of the *Milo* — coiling with muscular energy, and a thinner, silky type which is either pleated or arranged in a flurry of crisscrossing, sharp ridges. These textural differentiations underline a clear definition of details and planes, which is extended beyond the drapery to the areas of hair and flesh, and to the muscles of the representation of the *Belvedere Torso*, where marble imitates marble. Falconet shows a greater control over his chisel than he did in the *Milo*, and he qualifies his textures, his details, and his planes with a slight "melting" effect that safeguards them from the rather dry meticulousness prevailing in the earlier work. Thus, the crystalline grain of the marble substance is given its due, rather than being entirely sacrificed to the artist's concern with the imitation of reality; one seems to see the surface of the *Allegory* through a suggestion of a soft cloudy mist which somewhat recalls the sensuous *morbidezza* of the Italian Quattrocento.

The new interpretation of form is equally important. The *Allegory of Sculpture* is the first true example of Falconet's three-dimensional conception, in which the statue is meant to be seen from any angle. The *Milo*, with the figure placed against his tree, seems in contrast almost relief-like, a conception that confines the spectator to a fixed position, as with a painting. While the *Milo* can be characterized by what some German scholars call the *Spreizstil*, a style marked by openness and spreading, the *Allegory* is closer to the *Blockstil*, conveying a strong feeling of a concentrated solid mass.

The *Laocoön*, Bernini, and all the other Classical and Baroque references discerned in the *Milo of Crotona* disappear in the *Allegory of Sculpture* — the conception of this statue is dominated by one major source of inspiration: Michelangelo.

Falconet did not like Michelangelo's *Bacchus* and severely criticized his *Moses*. Nevertheless, he believed that Michelangelo's work was "awesome," and without praising him as much as Bernini or Puget, he nursed for him a great admiration. Michelangelo's influence is manifested first in the *contrapposto* of the *Allegory*. The major elements of Falconet's statue oppose one another around a central vertical axis. The head is turned to the right, the bust to the left, and the lower part of the body again to the right. The *contrapposto* is contrapuntally enriched with a three-dimensional radial theme, particularly noticeable at the base of the statue, where projecting volumes, such as the figure's left foot, the hanging flap of the drapery, and the thighs of the antique *Torso*, alternate with voids. In contrast to the over-complicated twisting of countless earlier statues of the Mannerist and the Baroque periods, Falconet's conception succeeds in bringing about a dramatic struggle of opposed thrusts while preserving an overall feeling of a coherently articulated, unified mass. The resulting heroic monumentality is definitely Michelangelesque.

It is difficult to pinpoint a specific source, for Falconet somewhat readapted the master of the Sistine Chapel to the taste of his own century (a situation that can be likened to an eighteenth-century French translation of Shakespeare). In his *Allegory*, the young sculptor failed to see the danger of a built-in stylistic dissonance where a too-sensuously mellow carving technique is applied to a dramatically energetic play of form. Moreover, despite her powerfully muscular arms, the young woman who personifies Sculpture is definitely lacking in *terribilità*. Her soft oval face (Fig. 11) does not recall Michelangelo, but rather the mildly classicizing features often occuring in the seventeenth century, in the paintings of Lebrun and the sculptures of Girardon, for example.

Yet it is impossible to deny that the *Allegory's* heroic attitude and its corresponding feeling of an almost rebellious, self-asserting pride directly echo a particular type of Michelangelo — a type recurring in his art and which can best be illustrated by the *Delphic Sybil* of the Sistine Chapel (Fig. 10). It is important to note that the eighteenth century had little affinity for Michelangelo, and that the great Florentine master never came to be adopted as a popular model by the French artists of the Rococo era. From this point of view, Falconet's Michelangelism constitutes a most interesting phenomenon.

It is evident that in *Milo of Crotona* and in the *Allegory of Sculpture*, Falconet tried to satisfy his Academic judges. He also tried to capture the attention of the Salon public by displaying his originality through an acute kind of pathos, in the case of *Milo*, and through Michelangelism, in the case of the *Allegory*. Soon after becoming an *agréé*, Falconet came to realize that a spirit of compliancy was more useful than originality in obtaining profitable commissions. This fact was particularly compelling to a young artist trying his wings, and in spite of his philosophical rigorism, the Jean-Jacques of sculpture had to accept the bitter necessity of pleasing his patrons. Falconet's first important commission, *France Embracing the Bust of Louis XV* (Fig. 12), can be best understood in this context.

It was one of the works assigned to various artists by the *Directeur des Bâtiments*, Le Normant de Tournehem, to commemorate the king's recovery from a serious illness with which he had been stricken in 1744. To obtain his first royal commission (probably in 1745), Falconet consented to base his composition on a drawing provided by Charles Coypel, the *premier peintre du roi*. Such subordination of a sculptor to a painter was far from exceptional, for the custom had been well established in the seventeenth century by the painter Charles Lebrun in his relations with the sculptors of Versailles. Falconet was granted the honor of a special Louvre studio, and all-in-all, for a young struggling sculptor, this situation was more auspicious than humiliating.

Everything went well at the beginning. The preliminary terra-cotta, shown in the Salon of 1747, was soon followed by a full-size plaster model, which appeared in the exhibition of the succeeding year. The sculptor eventually grew tired of this work, however, and after seventeen years, in 1762, he requested to be excused from the commission, offering to reimburse the 9050 *livres* he had received on account. In writing to Marigny, *Directeur des Bâtiments* at this time, he describes his group as a "very bad model" that he had agreed to execute when he was still a young man, under "the dictation" of the first painter to the king, in order to satisfy pressing financial needs. The commission was reassigned to Edmé Dumont, and after Dumont's death to Augustin Pajou, who completed the marble carving of the group in 1779.

Commemorating a minor episode of the life of a rather disreputable monarch, this largish monument (about 5 feet) is at present relegated to a corridor in the city hall of the provincial town of Libourne (Fig. 12). Its iconography is based on stereotypes. The personification of France, wearing a mantle adorned with fleurs-de-lis, is eagerly reaching up to embrace an armor-clad bust of Louis XV, mounted on a column that symbolizes eternity. The scheme is completed with a variety of allegorical details, such as a shield, palm leaves, and a cornucopia, that suitably allude to the king's accomplishments in war and peace.

Because of this subject, the 1747 terra-cotta enjoyed a moderate *succès d'estime* among the Salon critics. Obviously too many artists were eventually involved for the final work to give any clear idea of Falconet's own contribution. Some details, such as the Greek key design of the cushion placed under the figure of France, and her braided hairdo, are still reminiscent of the *Allegory of Sculpture*. The persistence of the sculptor's earlier style is also felt in the deeply carved and ridged, powerfully "muscular" drapery of France's mantle; when seen from the back (Fig. 13), it reveals a stately sweep that evokes the sumptuously cloaked funeral statues of the sixteenth and seventeenth centuries. In general, Falconet's group gives a feeling of Baroque ponderousness, which is probably why the Salon critics were inspired to write that the sculptor should have given his conception an "antique air." But considering the above mentioned predicaments, one must recognize that the work retains a great degree of energy and that the attitude of the figure of France — reminiscent of the attitude of the corresponding allegory in Rubens's *Arrival of Marie de Médicis in Marseilles* (Louvre) — combines Baroque ponderousness with a good measure of Baroque vitality.

The turning point in these early Baroque tendencies is represented by the statue of *Music* (Fig. 14). This large work (about 6 feet), now in the Louvre, is a landmark in the artist's career, for it was executed for Madame de Pompadour's newly built château of Bellevue (completed in 1750), and it was Falconet's first important Pompadour commission. The statue was indeed in good company. It was part of the magnificent Bellevue ensemble that included works of painters such as Oudry, Carle van Loo, and Boucher, and sculptors such as Adam, Saly, Coustou, and Pigalle.

A small plaster model for *Music* (about 26 inches) was exhibited, with some success, in the Salon of 1751. The final marble statue, for which the sculptor received the handsome sum of 10,000 *livres*, was probably completed in 1752. The statue had the unusual good luck to survive, almost unscathed, the Revolutionary vandalism that befell Bellevue, as well as the fire that destroyed the château of Saint-Cloud, where it was brought after the Revolution.

Crowned with laurels and holding a lyre, Falconet's figure is based on a simplified conception of the traditional allegory of Music and of the corresponding Muse, Euterpe. The only notable iconographic particularity of the statue is the score of Lagarde's opera *Eglé*, placed at its feet. This detail is a direct homage to Madame de Pompadour, who had triumphed in the leading role of the opera when it was performed, for the first time, at Versailles, in 1750.

Music seems to stand on the front of a stage, singing for an unseen audience whose presence is suggested by the direction of her gaze and the declamatory quality of her gesture (Figs. 14-15) — this is the very psychological device used in Bernini's *Longinus*, in Saint Peter's. The Baroque conception is also reflected in the size and in the strength of the figure, while at the same time an ornamental Rococo quality finds its way into her graceful *déhanchement* and in the elegant rumpling of her drapery *à la Boucher* (the drapery still marked by the ridges of Falconet's earlier style). Yet these Baroque and Rococo factors cannot hide a new feeling of idealization and clarity. It is far too early to speak of Classicism in any "Neoclassical" sense, but one has the impression that Falconet is finding a new style, which is beginning to take shape in the midst of the earlier emotional and decorative bravura.

III

From Lucidity Louis XV to the Classical Problem

IN SPEAKING about the eighteenth century, it is traditional to point out that seldom before had literature and art reached such a degree of closeness — never before had the Horatian *Ut pictura poesis* found such eloquent justification. To limit oneself to most obvious examples, it can be shown that the subjects of Greuze's painting are permeated with the spirit of the *drame bourgeois* and that the turgid tragedies of Voltaire parallel the late Baroque theatricality of Carle van Loo's art. The Horatian principle, however, has limitations. For instance, the literary achievements of the eighteenth century are associated with the concept of Enlightenment, while its artistic productions tend in general to be equated with the Rococo style. Surprisingly enough, there has been little attempt to explain how the precision, the clarity, and the common sense that characterize the major writing of this period — from Montesquieu to Diderot — are supposed to be mirrored in the capricious visual paradoxes of what is usually designated as the Rococo style. A comparison between literature and art naturally involves a great variety of factors, but if one confines oneself to the question of stylistic structure, it may be admitted that it is most difficult to reconcile the luminous logic of a sentence of Voltaire (outside his unfortunate tragedies) with the arbitrary convolutions of Boucher's painting.

It is true that something of the clarity of eighteenth-century writers is present in Louis Quinze architecture; it is very much a part, for example, of Servandoni's facade of Saint-Sulpice or Gabriel's Petit Trianon, which hardly succumb to Rococo ornamentation. It is also true that in a very different manner, rationalism governs an important aspect of the eighteenth-century naturalism, that developed in Chardin's painting. Such illustrations, however, tend to be special cases, and on the whole, the visual art of the first half of the eighteenth century — bathing in the echoes of the late Baroque and of the Rococo — was yet to create a style which would parallel the work of the great writers in its lucidity. Eventually, toward the end of the century, the question will find a glacial Neoclassical answer in the application of the credo of Winckelmann and his disciples, but one must keep in mind that this question was already in the air before the spread of the passion for the Antique. Needless to say, Falconet never surrendered his art either to the realm of pure logic or to full-fledged *antiquomanie;* but the changing aesthetic climate created by these elements must be taken into account to understand the nature of what might be called *lucidity Louis XV* — Falconet's new style emerging in the 1750's.

A statue of Cupid, generally known as *The Menacing Cupid (L'Amour menaçant),* offers the first important example of this style (Figs. 16, 19). Following a plaster model, which remained almost unnoticed in the exhibition of 1755, the finished marble *Cupid* was entered in the Salon of 1757, where it was received with fervent praise: the critics unanimously admired the subtlety of the artist's interpretation and the life-like quality of the execution. Naturally this enthusiastic acclaim had been spurred by the fact that the statue was intended for the Hôtel d'Evreux (today the Palais de l'Elysée), one of Madame de Pompadour's residences in Paris. There was no real need, however, for any artificial encouragement by the critics, for the *Cupid* enjoyed — and still enjoys — a spectacular success. It was reproduced innumerable times, in marble, in bronze, and biscuit. Several of the early replicas were executed by Falconet himself — the original work (about 35 inches) is probably the marble in the Louvre (Fig. 16) — and they were followed by copies of various sizes, multiplied by legions of imitators and forgers, through the eighteenth, nineteenth, and even the twentieth centuries. *Cupid's* popularity is also reflected in its appearance in a number of eighteenth-century paintings, such as Fragonard's *Hasards heureux de l'escarpolette* (1768, Wallace Collection) and Roslin's *Jeune Fille offrant des fleurs à l'Amour* (1783, Louvre).

Art and literature overflow with Cupids, and this overabundance can be a source of confusion. A case in point is provided by a couplet of Voltaire, which frequently appears on copies of Falconet's *Cupid:*

> Qui que tu sois, voici ton maître
> Il l'est, le fut ou le doit être.

One must note, with a twinge of disappointment, that this bit of poetry was composed independently of the statue, and that its charming variation on the Vergilian *love conquers all* has no direct relation with Falconet's subject.

More importantly, one must realize that the very title traditionally attached to the statue, *The Menacing Cupid,* is as apocryphal as it is misleading. The gesture of the little god, who brings his right forefinger to his mouth, does not convey the idea of menace, but rather that of silence. It is evidently derived from one of the many representations of Harpocrates, the god of silence (Fig. 17), or from the theme of *discreet love,* exemplified by the Cupid of Luca Giordano's *Sleep of Endymion* (Verona). Apparently Falconet's conception spurred a revival of this old theme, as can be seen in the Cupids which appear in Noël Hallé's painting of *Hippomenes and Atalante* (1765, Louvre) and in Jean-Baptiste Lemoyne's sculptural group of *Vertumnus and Pomona* (1760, Louvre; Fig. 18). However, Falconet's conception is more complex, and the theme of Cupid's silencing gesture is enriched with the kind of Anacreontic refinements that so often preside over eighteenth-century *amours* (Bouchardon's famous *Cupid* of 1739, for instance, was shown in the process of carving his bow out of the wood of Hercules' club, using the weapons of Mars as tools). The novelty of Falconet's idea was to involve the viewer in his subject. Looking down from his marble cloud, the god of love with one hand seems to ask the onlooker to remain still, while with the other he is surreptitiously pulling an arrow from his quiver: the *Cupid* requests our complicity to better surprise his intended victim.

The *Cupid* is the first major representation of a child in Falconet's art. Superficially, the statue recalls the countless Cupids characteristic of Boucher and of other eighteenth-century artists, but a closer examination reveals a significant difference of age. The sculptor breaks with the tradition of showing the god of love either as an adolescent or as an infant: his child is not an adolescent, but he is perceptibly older than the typical cherubs and *amours* of Boucher: he is a little boy about six years old. He has definitely outgrown the *putto* stage and does not belong to the breed of the fleshy — almost swollen — little *putti* frolicking through Rococo art. Escaping eighteenth-century formulas, Falconet chose to portray the growing-out-of-babyhood stage. Because he preferred to depict a somewhat older child, the attitude and the gestures of his figure acquire a naturalness seldom seen in the precocious infant-Cupids of the time. The result is convincingly realistic. However, this realism is not allowed to become agressive, and it is tempered by nuances of tenderness, idealization, and grace that are brought into a delicate balance. This subtlety is also felt in *Cupid's* facial expression — unexpectedly recalling that of Falconet in his bust by Mademoiselle Collot (Fig. 3) — which is playfully arch without becoming cute or saccharine.

The appearance of a new type is accompanied by the appearance of a new concept of sculptural form. Admittedly, Falconet does not divorce himself totally from the stylistic vocabulary of the earlier eighteenth century, and every line of the *Cupid* constitutes an episode of a sustained undulation that seems to pulsate from curls to toes. But the Rococo rhythm is kept under control and is not allowed to blur the articulation of forms. Without ever becoming truly geometrical, the volumes of the statue are endowed with a clearly defined individual existence. Their interrelation shows neither the jerky angularity of the *Milo* (Fig. 6), nor the dramatic twisting of the *Allegory of Sculpture* (Fig. 9), and the three-dimensional elements of the figure, opposed one against another, are brought to a harmonic equilibrium in a succession of undramatic contrasts. Falconet's compositional understatement is evolved in the context of a lucidity of vision, which is felt in the crisp precision of details, such as arrows and roses, as well as in the clarity of form of the statue as a whole.

The year 1757 is one of the most pleasant landmarks in Falconet's career. The success of the *Cupid* was equalled by the success of *The Bather*, which was also shown in the Salon of 1757 and was praised in almost identical terms. The original small marble statue (about 32 inches) is now in the Louvre (Figs. 20, 21, 22). Like the *Cupid*, *The Bather* came to be reproduced countless times — in marble, bronze, lead, and biscuit — from the eighteenth century to the modern period (a commercially multiplied diminutive plaster version found its way even to the slopes of the Acropolis). The best-known of the *Bather* replicas, *The Bather with the Rose* (Fig. 23) in the Victoria and Albert Museum, shows slight variations from the original and can probably be ascribed to Falconet himself. Despite the fact that at the time of its Salon exhibition *The Bather* was owned by a comparatively obscure *homme de robe*, Thiroux d'Espersennes, the popularity of the statue grew to the point of playing a lasting influence on the court fashions; thus, as late as 1775, Pajou executed a bust of Madame du Barry, the new favorite of the king, with her hair arranged "in the manner of Falconet's Bather."

Among the multitude of bathers produced through centuries of art — their number nearly matches the number of Cupids — the statue of Falconet asserts itself through interesting innovations and a definite aesthetic individuality. While most of the earlier bathers are shown after their bath, Falconet is one of the very few sculptors since Praxiteles, in his celebrated *Aphrodite of Cnidus*, to have depicted the moment before. His *Bather*, or *Nymph* (as the statue is described in the catalogue of the 1757 Salon), is about to step into her bath. Leaning on a tree trunk and holding a chemise, she seems to feel with the tip of her foot the coolness of the water. The subject was probably derived from a painting by François Lemoyne (unrelated to Falconet's teacher), which shows a bather in a very similar attitude (Fig. 25). Lemoyne's *Bather* (1724) was often copied (for example, replicas in Tours and Leningrad), and its reproduction appears on a vase produced by the Sèvres factory that employed Falconet.

Falconet's *Bather* has little to do with mythology. The choice of this particular genre theme merely gave the artist the opportunity to represent a beautiful young girl in a graceful momentary pose — the viewer's anticipation of her touching the cool water surface almost suggests a quivering in the marble. This fugitive element adds a poetic note to a figure, which, like the *Cupid*, depicts a transitional age of human life, adolescence on the brink of womanhood. In comparison with this subtle dosage of vulnerability and eroticism, the other bathers of the second half of the eighteenth century, such as Boizot's *Bathing Nymph* of 1774 (Fig. 24; Victoria and Albert Museum), appear to be almost matronly and common. With Falconet's *Bather*, French sculpture acknowledges for the first time *la femme-enfant*, a type which also asserts itself compellingly amidst the century's *dramatis personae* with Prévost's *Manon Lescaut* and Greuze's *Cruche cassée*.

The nude *Bather's* chaste hairdo, small head, drooping shoulders, and amphora-like silhouette are marked with the seal of the blasé refinements of the Louis XV era. This voluptuously mannered elegance is also expressed in the attitude of the figure, bending forward with a coquettishly emphatic hip movement that recalls the *déhanchement* of some medieval statues. Yet *The Bather* is much more than a dainty, erotic marble figurine: the articulations of the body are organically defined, the muscles "work," and the texture of the flesh has a softness and an elasticity that are effectively brought out by a contrast with the crisp ridges of the rhythmically crumpled drapery — the artist worked from life and probably used Mademoiselle Mistouflet, his mistress at the time, as a model.

The Bather is no more an anatomical study than it is a pretty Rococo doll. In this statue, as in the *Cupid*, the sculptor, avoiding naturalistic overstatements, remained constantly concerned with the crystalline immaculateness of his material and with the clarity of his sculptural forms. Falconet's concern with purity as well as the controlled precision of his carving brings about a quality of "frosty" remoteness — a touch of ethereality — which creates a psychological distance between the viewer and the statue. This quality should not be confused with inertness. A dance-like balancing of arms and legs endows *The Bather*, equipoised on the apex of its vase-like shape, with the tensile energy of a bending bow. Because of Falconet's sense of form, this charming genre figure, which could have been merely graceful, has become lucid and lyrically dynamic.

Four years after *The Bather*, the statue of *Sweet Melancholy* (Figs. 26 and 27) marked the appearance of a far-reaching stylistic development. There is little doubt that Falconet was convinced of the importance of this work, for he entered it three times in the Salon: in 1761, as a plaster model, and in 1763 and in 1765 in its finished marble form (marble now in the Hermitage). The statue (about 39 inches) was greatly admired for the simple grace of its contour and the subtly touching quality of its expression. In his 1765 *Salon*, Diderot reports some minor criticisms of the exaggerated roundness of the figure's right arm and of the heaviness of the lower part of the drapery. But he attributes these adverse comments to other authors, and they do not prevent him from expressing his enthusiasm for Falconet's ability to capture most elusive emotions.

Sweet Melancholy was commissioned by La Live de Jully, one of Falconet's most loyal patrons. The identity of the patron, however, is hardly sufficient reason to follow Réau in assuming that the elegiac theme of the statue alluded to the death of La Live de Jully's wife: the statue was conceived in 1761, and the death of the patron's wife had occurred nine years before, in 1752, and had already been commemorated, in 1753, in a tomb designed by Falconet (see Chap. V). As a subject, *melancholy* — particularly, *sweet melancholy* — was becoming extremely fashionable around 1760. It corresponded to the affectation of teary sensibility that increasingly pervaded the second half of the century. Appearing the year of the publication of Rousseau's *Nouvelle Héloïse*, the bedside book of *âmes sensibles*, Falconet's *Sweet Melancholy* echoed the popularity of a major eighteenth-century pre-Romantic trend.

Eighteenth-century manifestations of sensibility took a number of forms. Thus, the dove that appears in Falconet's statue gives it a characteristically Pompadour flavor — the Marquise had a great affection for this species. In *Sweet Melancholy*, however, the Pompadour spirit is far less important than the expression of a new classical mode. Classicism permeates the statue, in the architectural details of the column on which the figure leans, in her chiton-like drapery and Grecian coiffure, in her idealized features and the elongated S-curve of her silhouette. The Classical influence is so conspicuous that it raises the question of direct borrowing from a Greek or a Roman prototype. The curiously crowded linear pattern of the lower portion of the drapery seems to point to a derivation from an engraving reproducing a Classical relief, such as the *Sarcophagus of the Muses* (Louvre).

A borrowing of this kind can explain the quasi-antiquarian effect produced by *Sweet Melancholy*. The specifically Classical quality of the figure's sinuous contour, the "liquid" treatment of her drapery, and the idealization of her features represent a deliberate departure from the highly original stylistic conception that characterized the *Cupid* and *The Bather*.

Thus 1761 is a crucial date — it is the very date chosen by Jean Locquin, in his most authoritative *Peinture d'histoire en France de 1747 à 1785*, to identify the real beginning of Neoclassical tendencies in France. With *Sweet Melancholy*, Falconet becomes directly involved in a problem that combines the emerging eighteenth-century pre-Romantic sensibility with the increasingly pervasive eighteenth-century antiquarianism. He will have to reconcile these new factors with the natural growth of his own artistic instinct. In this context, antiquarianism — which was rapidly turning into antiquomania — is particularly important. While it is futile to decide on the relative attractiveness of the *Bather* and *Sweet Melancholy*, it is certain that the latter, because of its assumed Classicism, has lost something of the vitality and of the compositional energy so evident in the *Bather*. It is interesting to note that Pigalle, Falconet's chief competitor, spent three years in Rome at the very beginning of his career and made direct copies from the antique, such as his *Knucklebone Player* (1738), without any significant consequences to the development of his own style. Falconet came to be actively concerned with the Classical mode much later in the century, at the time he had already succeeded in clarifying and revitalizing the Rococo formulas on his own terms. Until the end of his creative career, the sculptor will struggle to absorb the Classical influence without destroying his hard-won stylistic identity. This struggle will remain the major problem of his later artistic development.

The first telling signs of Falconet's dilemma in confronting Classicism as a problem become apparent in 1763, in the group of *Pygmalion and Galatea*. The work, known today through two major examples, a small version (about $22\frac{1}{2}$ inches) in the Walters Art Gallery (Fig. 28) and a larger version (about 33 inches) in the Louvre (Fig. 30), marks the apogee of his Salon success. The subject of the statue was anything but new. Generally following Ovid's *Metamorphoses*, the artist represented the well-known story of the sculptor Pygmalion falling in love with the statue he had just finished; the statue, later given the name of Galatea, comes to life through a miraculous intervention of Cupid, the agent of Aphrodite. The theme had already inspired scores of poems, stage performances, and works of art. It is possible that the execution of Falconet's *Pygmalion* was prompted by the popularity of a ballet by Rameau (performed in 1748, 1751, 1752, and 1760), and it is probable that the basic idea of the composition was derived from a painting (1729) of the same subject by François Lemoyne (Tours; Fig. 29).

Before he became known as the sculptor of *Peter the Great*, Falconet was known as the sculptor of *Pygmalion* — none of his previous productions had enjoyed a comparable triumph among the critics. Their praises were specially directed at three aspects which are pointed out in a lyrical page of Diderot's *Salon* of 1763, where the philosopher goes so far as to compare the artist to Phidias and to Prometheus. Diderot applauds the realism of a work, in which one can see "three different kinds of flesh" corresponding to the three figures of the group. He admires the simultaneous depiction of several different passions in the single figure of Pygmalion: "surprise, joy, and love blended together." Finally, he extols the sculptor's eloquent suggestion of the appearance of the first signs of life and of the "first thought" in a marble statue that is becoming a woman.

It is difficult today to be greatly impressed by the degree of realism found in this particular work of Falconet; one is no longer affected by the appearance of three different emotions in a same figure; and nobody could earnestly admire the birth of Galatea's "first thought" without thinking of Michelangelo's *Creation of Man* or of Rodin's *Bronze Age*. In the twentieth century, one's admiration of Falconet's group is inspired by other factors. Far from being moved by the dramatic power of this miracle of love, one is touched by the delightfully naïve theatricality of the protagonists. Thus the clenched hands and the radiant look of Pygmalion (Fig. 32) evoke the enthusiastic insincerity of an actor performing a scene from an opera by Rameau or Mozart. Despite its two-dimensional organization, Falconet's composition is as forceful as it is decorative. It has the dynamics of an exploding Roman candle — an effect that is especially noticeable in the back view of the group — with diverging and converging curved trajectories initiated in each one of the figures (Fig. 34). It can be readily acknowledged with Diderot, of course, that Falconet's group is a "precious thing," and it is possible to add that its delicate precision and its artificiality make one think of a lovingly wrought *objet de luxe*.

This expression is used here without any disparaging intention, for Falconet's *Pygmalion* represents a high level of intellectual and aesthetic achievement, and it is a work of art of some stylistic complexity. One aspect of this complexity is reflected in the sculptor's groping effort to find his own working approach to the already mentioned "Classical problem." Diderot had a premonition of the problem when he contrasted the figure of Galatea with that of Pygmalion and indicated that he preferred the former.

Falconet's Galatea (Fig. 31) shows an unmistakable resemblance to his *Bather*. However, while she repeats, in a general manner, the *Bather's* physical type and attitude, she also reveals appreciable differences. Galatea depicts a somewhat older woman, her proportions are heavier, and her figure is less supple and more static. Conceived in far less Classical terms than *Sweet Melancholy*, Galatea shows nevertheless the artist's attempt to modify the type of the earlier *Bather* with a suggestion of Classical idealism and Classical quiescence (these qualities are particularly in evidence in the Louvre version).

The other figures of Falconet's group display diametric tendencies. The capricious, corkscrewed clouds, the agile, putto-like Cupid, and the almost acrobatically mannered and gaping Pygmalion openly proclaim their Rococo affiliation. This contrast can be justified by the requirements of the subject: a marble statue coming to life would logically be more restrained — from every point of view — than the figure of its sculptor or that of a miracle-performing Cupid. Nonetheless, this contrast exists, and transcending the question of iconography, it marks the beginning of a stylistic polarity. Thus, Galatea becomes more Classical, and Pygmalion more Rococo; the very nature of Falconet's subject matter led him, in this case, to adopt an approach to the "Classical problem" that is based essentially not on a stylistic absorption but rather on a stylistic coexistence.

The "Classical problem" completely dominates Falconet's entries to the Salon of 1765 (Fig. 33). It was his last Salon — he was about to embark on his Russian venture — and it was marred by some disappointment, for the critics, including Diderot, gave only a lukewarm reception to *Apelles and Campaspe*, Falconet's major piece in the exhibition (Fig. 35). This work, despite its comparatively small size (about $33 \times 27\frac{1}{4}$ inches), was the most important relief ever produced by the sculptor, but it did not quite succeed in upholding the standard of success established by *Pygmalion and Galatea*.

The story of Apelles and Campaspe was narrated by several Classical authors. Most probably the artist based his subject on a passage of Book XXXV of Pliny the Elder's *Naturalis historia*, which he translated seven years later. One day Alexander the Great ordered Apelles to paint Campaspe, the most beloved of his concubines. Because of her extraordinary beauty, the artist was asked to portray her in the nude. Realizing that

Apelles, in obeying his command, had fallen in love with Campaspe, Alexander gave her to him: "not less admirable for this action than for any of his victories, since he conquered himself."

The vagueness of this pseudo-historical anecdote forced Falconet to invent every detail of the scene, which, according to the Salon catalogue, he situated at the very moment when the monarch was giving his mistress to his painter. The setting suggests palatial surroundings with arches and pilasters. Facing Campaspe, who is propped against cushions and draperies, Apelles is seated in front of an easel with a large canvas on which appear the outlines of his projected painting. Standing behind his favorite, Alexander seems to urge her toward the painter, while two spear-carrying guards are looking on.

In his *Salon* of 1765, Diderot was disturbed by the paradox of what he considered a too-virginal-looking Campaspe, as well as by the implausibility of the two soldiers being allowed to witness such a ticklish moment. Falconet himself did not take the story too seriously. Unimpressed by its equivocal morality, he considered the subject mainly as a traditional glorification of the art of painting. In this sense, the theme parallels that of *Pygmalion*, which is essentially a glorification of sculpture.

Such an attitude toward the subject could hardly stimulate a very moving interpretation: the scene is acted out in a most predictable pantomime that recalls scores of conventional renditions of comparable emotional situations in art. But this conspicuous lack of spontaneity has still another reason. In *Apelles and Campaspe*, Falconet, expanding his earlier experience of *Sweet Melancholy*, tried to be as Classical as he could. Showing his awareness of Winckelmann, whose writings were becoming increasingly known in France, the sculptor strove to endow his figures with what he thought constituted the noble restraint of Antiquity. Naturally he also multiplied pseudo-antiquarian touches, such as the regally crested helmet of Alexander and the emphatically plebeian tunic of Apelles. This attempts at Classicism, based chiefly on more or less reliable secondary sources, did not prevent the artist from grouping his figures in a manner that, as Diderot noted, brings to mind the composition of *Pygmalion*. As a consequence, Campaspe emerges as a second, and somewhat duller, reincarnation of the *Bather*, and the scheme of the relief gives a feeling of *déjà vu* Academism.

But *Apelles and Campaspe* involves a far more important aspect of the "Classical problem." Falconet's approach to Classicism was marked by a curious ambivalence. To him, the art of the Ancients stimulated a spirit of rivalry more than one of imitation. From this point of view, *Apelles and Campaspe* gave the artist an opportunity to illustrate some of the ideas he had previously discussed in his *Réflexions sur la sculpture* (see translation in Appendix) — ideas that, according to him, offered a way to improve upon the unsatisfactory reliefs produced by Ancient art.

Remembering Leonardo's celebrated parallel of painting and sculpture — unfavorable to sculpture — Falconet contended that with the exception of the question of color, the problems posed by a high relief were basically the same as the problems posed by a painting: both techniques follow identical principles aimed at imitating nature. The inferences of this guiding maxim, in his view so sadly ignored by the Ancients, are developed in *Apelles and Campaspe*. Approaching his relief in a painter-like fashion,

Falconet strove to create the illusion of three-dimensional space. Thus, to avoid the effect of what he called "cut-out figures pasted on a board," he systematically applied the rules of aerial and linear perspective. The figures of Apelles and Campaspe, in the foreground, show considerable precision and appear to be almost detached from the marble plane. As forms recede in space, details become increasingly vague, and the projection of the relief slowly diminishes and nearly disappears in the background, where the architecture is depicted in a faint, linear pattern. At the same time, figures decrease in size from the foreground to the background, and parallel lines converge toward calculated vanishing points.

Falconet did not quite succeed in showing — as he maintains in his *Réflexions* — that the sculptor of a relief can suggest color by varying the roughness and the polish of the marble surface, but on the whole he thoroughly demonstrated his theory. Stylistically this demonstration, which brings to mind a *Beaux-Arts* exercise, lies between Baroque illusionism and the formal purification that will be forthcoming in the Neoclassical approach.

In the Salon of 1765, another, quite different, example of Falconet's Classical mode could be seen in his allegory of *Friendship*. This marble statue (39 inches) is often called *Friendship with the Heart* (*l'Amitié au coeur*), to distinguish it from the sculptor's earlier biscuit Friendships (Figs. 37, 94). (The location of the marble is presently unknown,[7] and consequently it is represented here by its biscuit version at Sèvres, Fig. 36.)

The theme of friendship is characteristically late *Pompadour*. Around 1750, after the end of her love affair with Louis XV, the Marquise, who had retained all her political influence, made a special effort to publicize the new platonic nature of her attachment to the king. The theme of friendship became known as the unofficial emblem of Madame de Pompadour, and Falconet and several other artists (including Pigalle) took part in what had the appearance of a campaign of moral rehabilitation through friendship.

In Falconet's *Friendship with the Heart*, as well as in most of the Friendships of this period, the elements of the allegory were derived from the famous, endlessly re-edited late-sixteenth-century *Iconologia* of Cesare Ripa and from the series of emblematic engravings executed under the direction of the Marquise (*ca.* 1752). These sources explain the heart held by Falconet's figure, her bare arms and feet (friendship's willingness to withstand hardship), her crown of myrtle leaves and pomegranate flowers (union of wills in friendship), the mask lying at her feet (friendship's rejection of hypocrisy), and the dry elm stump entwined with vine on which she is leaning (friendship survives changes of fortune). Thus from the iconographic point of view this figure is very similar to other eighteenth-century Friendships. The most unusual single element of Falconet's statue is, of course, her gesture of offering her heart with both hands. This votive gesture and the general attitude of the figure do not follow the tradition of the allegory of Friendship, and they seem to have been influenced by Urania, another of Ripa's emblems (Fig. 38). Falconet replaced the Muse Urania's crown of stars with leaves and flowers, and her celestial globe with a heart.

[7] A small photograph of the marble statue appears in Diderot's *Salons* edited by J. Seznec and J. Adhémar (Oxford: Clarendon Press, 1960), II, Pl. 78. In this work, Falconet's *Friendship* is described as belonging to the collection of Edmond de Rothschild.

A few critics castigated the literalism of this anatomical attribute, but the majority admired the sensitivity of the conception. In his *Salon* of 1765, Diderot states that in Falconet's *Friendship with the Heart*, there is much more pathos than in a painting by Greuze, and he finds that the head of the statue shows an "undefinable feeling of enthusiasm and sacredness" that he has never encountered before.

Even a jaded twentieth-century viewer could not cursorily dismiss Falconet's work as saccharine. It is undeniably sentimental, but it is subtly ennobled by a radiant expression of tenderness and fervor which recalls the mystical overtones of some of the figures of Fragonard's *Coresus and Callirhoé* (Louvre), exhibited in the same Salon. With this statue, Falconet captures an ephemeral note of the 1760's, bringing into consonance pre-Romantic and pre-Classical trends. One cannot minimize the Classical significance of this work. With its willowy grace and its silky, "liquid" drapery, the *Friendship with the Heart* is a close kin of the 1761 *Sweet Melancholy*, but it is free from the obvious eclecticism that characterizes the earlier statue. It is Falconet's most successful and most appealing attempt to find a personal solution to the "Classical problem."

Falconet's terra-cotta model of the figure of *Winter*, exhibited in the same Salon of 1765, doubtless reflected an equal preoccupation with Classicism. The terra-cotta has disappeared, but this preoccupation can be seen clearly in the finished marble statue (about $4\frac{1}{2}$ feet) now in the Hermitage (Figs. 39-42). Falconet's allegory of *Winter* has a long and complicated history. It was ordered in 1763 by Madame de Pompadour. But after her death, in 1764, the commission was taken over by the Marquis de Marigny, who intended to place the statue — then still only a project — in the botanical gardens of the Petit Trianon. Because of technical mishaps, the work on the marble had hardly begun at the time of Falconet's departure for Russia. Before leaving France, the sculptor bought back his statue from Marigny and sent it to Saint Petersburg, where he completed the carving (1771) and resold the finished *Winter* to Catherine II.

The iconography of *Winter* is far from the familiar tradition of the shivering, fur-clad personifications of that season. According to the catalogue of the Salon of 1765, the female figure of *Winter* was intended to be placed in the midst of a bed of winter-flowering plants. The allegory was conceived in the simplest possible manner, with this purpose in mind. Besides winter flowers, its attributes include only a vase, which has burst from the freezing of the water it contains, and the signs of Capricorn and of Aquarius, depicted on the seat. The novelty of this iconography is the depiction of Winter as a kind of greenhouse divinity who, with a gesture analogous to that of a medieval *Virgin of Pity*, protects winter flowers with a fold of her drapery.

The terra-cotta model of *Winter* was praised in the Salon of 1765 for the delicate beauty of its form-revealing drapery and the illusionism of its vase broken by the frost. Writing to Marigny the same year, Falconet stated that he believed it was the best statue he could ever hope to conceive. For several critics, like Diderot and Jean-Baptiste Claude Robin, *Winter* was especially praiseworthy because of its antique character. In fact, it appears almost certain that Falconet derived his idea from a Classical representation of a seated female figure, such as the Hellenistic *Fortune of Antioch* (Vatican).

Winter parallels the trend initiated in *Apelles and Campaspe*. Admittedly, the statue is free from the technical pedantry displayed in the relief, but the careful ordering of the semicircular folds of its drapery, its rounded contours, and the studied simplicity of its compact mass point to the same self-conscious concern with an ideal of "noble" Classicism. Like *Apelles and Campaspe, Winter* represents a perceptible step in the direction of Neo-classical sculpture. Nevertheless, one cannot deny that Falconet's latest effort to master the "Classical problem" reveals a number of echoes of his earlier style. The serene grace, the quiet eroticism, and particularly the facial expression of the figure of *Winter* (Fig. 41), with her chastely downcast eyes and tender half-smile, unmistakably recall the feminine type of the *Bather*.

It is difficult to establish an accurate chronology of the Classical experimentations of Falconet. It appears that the sculptor simultaneously explored the possibilities of two parallel Classicizing stylistic trends. The first is exemplified by *Sweet Melancholy* and *Friendship with the Heart*, and the second by *Apelles and Campaspe* and *Winter*. The former trend is characterized by a soft, almost "liquid" suppleness and a sensuous pre-Romantic sentimentality, while the latter is an attempt to capture the spirit and the form of puristic antiquarianism. These two trends — one is tempted to call them Ionic and Doric — are rooted in the style of *lucidity Louis XV*, which reached it apogee in the *Cupid* and in the *Bather*. The important Rococo manifestations occurring — at the "wrong time" — in *Pygmalion and Galatea* eloquently demonstrate that this stylistic evolution was anything but mechanical or predictable.

IV

Biscuits and Statuettes

THE TEN YEARS of Falconet's association with Sèvres (1757-1766) coincided with the golden age of this prestigious ceramic center. The year prior to his appointment the entire factory had moved from Vincennes to its new location at Sèvres, halfway between Paris and Versailles, flatteringly close to Madame de Pompadour's Château of Bellevue. When the sculptor joined the enterprise, it was already enjoying the patronage of the Marquise as well as the privileges attached to its title of *Manufacture Royale de Porcelaine de France*.

The artistic director of Sèvres was the painter Jean-Jacques Bachelier. He was responsible for the adoption of the *soft-paste* technique, which revolutionized the production of ceramic sculpture. Soft paste was a substitute for *hard paste*, the base of "true porcelain," which required the use of kaolin. In lieu of kaolin, a type of clay unavailable in France until the end of the reign of Louis XV, the technique of soft paste used diverse ingredients (sand from Fontainebleau, sea salt, saltpeter, soda alum, plaster of paris, etc.), which were treated and fired through a lengthy and difficult process. Soft paste was more fragile than hard paste. It was also less malleable, it did not lend itself well to painting, and it was easily scratched. But it produced a delicately unctuous, milky substance which was far more appealing to the eye than the raw white hard paste. Because of this quality, it was an ideal material for biscuit figures, which were modeled and fired without any application of glaze or color. Devoid of any kind of external embellishment, these biscuits demanded a great degree of precision from the sculptor. In a miniature scale (averaging 12 inches), they recalled some of the effects of marble sculpture, and they were characterized by a refinement of detail and a purity of form that could not be matched by the highly glazed and vividly painted products of the competing Meissen factory.

As director of the sculpture atelier, Falconet had the quasi-monopoly of the sculptural biscuit models supplied to Sèvres, and assisted by his pupils Duru and Le Riche he supervised the work of fifteen craftsmen. One knows nearly nothing, however, about the working relations between Falconet and his Sèvres assistants. This lack of information greatly complicates the problem of attribution: it is impossible to determine the extent of the sculptor's own contribution to the creation of biscuits, which always involved some participation from his assistants. One thing is certain: the biscuits that are associated in the archives of Sèvres with Falconet's name bear his approval by implication and, as such, must be accepted as representing his sculptural ideas. At a minimum, the significance of Falconet's name in those records is comparable to that of the label affixed to the creation of a *grand couturier*, or, to keep things in a proper context, to the significance of Rubens's signature on a canvas that required the extensive collaboration of other painters.

From this point of view, the aesthetic ascendancy of Falconet must be recognized in a number of biscuits that find their source in Boucher's compositions. A good example is offered by two companion pieces (1757): *The Magic Lantern* (Fig. 45) and *The Wafers Lottery* (Fig. 46). Admittedly, in both biscuits the general idea of the subject was borrowed from two different episodes of the *Country Fair*, a painting by Boucher popularized by an engraving of Cochin (Fig. 47). However, Falconet modified minor and major details, reduced the number of the figures, changed their ages, and gave them somewhat different expressions: in fact, he created two new groups.

In such borrowings, the passage from Boucher to Falconet was not limited to a change of details or a shift of mood. The transformation of a two-dimensional, single-view painting or drawing into a three-dimensional, many-sided sculptural composition could never have been accomplished in terms of literal matching. The effect of the creative imagination exercised by the sculptor in transforming a two-dimensional image can be seen in a comparison of two views of *The Teaching of Love*, another instance of a derivation from Boucher. Assuming that the frontal view of this biscuit (Fig. 43) is a fairly close rendition of a drawing (now lost), one must observe that the view from above (Fig. 44) shows a completely original organization of forms for which Boucher did not provide any model. Animated by a pattern of crisscross diagonals and pulsating nodules, this view brings to mind the capricious complexity of a strange living organism.

In stressing Falconet's originality, one should not discard the role of Boucher as insignificant. Until the very end of his career at Sèvres, the sculptor borrowed from the painter a variety of motifs that responded to the day-by-day commercial demands of the factory. This collaboration produced some unquestionable masterpieces, such as *The Teaching of Love* (1763) and *Jupiter and Leda* (Fig. 48; 1764). More often, however, Boucher's drawings supplied routinely charming compositions, like the *Schoolmistress* (Fig. 50; 1762) and the *Opera Dance* (Fig. 49; 1765), in which the painter's lack of inspiration was not always overcome by the sculptor.

Of course, Falconet was by no means limited to Boucher's prototypes. The sculptor's conceptions — like the conceptions of most artists — occasionally reveal a variety of art historical echoes, but such echoes should not be misconstrued as a mark of eclecticism. For instance, some of the figures of his *Silenus and the Bacchantes* (Fig. 51; 1759) suggest a distant kinship with Rubens (one thinks of a painting like *The Drunken Silenus*, in Munich). Yet this resemblance has no real significance, and it does not prevent the biscuit from being a magnificently individualistic expression of Falconet's art. In terms of plastic inventiveness, this group equals anything ever produced by the sculptor. Seen from above (Fig. 52), the sculptural mass shows a pattern of powerfully modeled, swelling spherical forms swept into a clockwise whirling motion. The biscuit has a throbbing, muscular, tactile quality that recalls the powerful immediacy of some of Barye's figures.

Falconet's most unchallengeably personal artistic commitment can be found in the biscuit renditions of some of his statues: *Cupid* (Fig. 16), *The Bather* (Fig. 20), *Sweet Melancholy* (Figs. 26, 27), *Pygmalion and Galatea* (Fig. 28), and *Friendship with the Heart* (Fig. 36). These biscuits were executed in two or three sizes (from 6 to 30 inches approximately), and often present minor variations from their marble models that can probably be ascribed to the sculptor's assistants. In the case of the Pygmalion group, for instance, some versions, properly trimmed with leaves, give a studiously chaster image of Galatea than the marble statue and include two Cupids instead of one. The smallness of these biscuits tends to give to them an additional feeling of refinement and fragility; and because of their precision, their diminutive scale unexpectedly underlines the realistic elements of Falconet's style. These qualities, more pronounced in some specimens than in others, can be illustrated in the beautiful *Cupid* of the Wallace Collection (Fig. 55).

It is certain that regardless of the role of his assistants, the sculptor made every effort to ensure the quality of the biscuits that were so obviously destined to popularize his Salon successes. Doubtless the same effort was extended to the companion pieces that were given to two such biscuits: the *Little Girl Hiding Cupid's Bow* (1761; Fig. 56), pendant to the *Cupid*, and the *Bather with a Sponge* (1762; Fig. 57), companion to the earlier *Bather*. Falconet, who conceived the biscuits of the *Little Girl* and of the new *Bather* independently of any of the marble models, had to make sure that they would hold their own in proximity to the biscuit reproductions of two of his most celebrated statues. One would expect that these companion pieces, which unavoidably required a special creative effort, bear the imprint of his stylistic "handwriting."

This hypothesis seems to be corroborated by the exceptional quality of these works. The *Little Girl Hiding Cupid's Bow* (occasionally called *Nymph* or *Psyche*) shares the characteristics of the *Cupid*, and also shows an increased sense of spontaneity and natural grace. The figure is a luminous expression of the very essence of the eighteenth century. The momentary charm, the youthful freshness, and the delicate suggestion of vulnerability of this biscuit undoubtedly played, a quarter of a century later, an influential role in some of Houdon's portrayals of children. Falconet fully realized the excellence of his *Little Girl*. Its plaster model (about 11 inches) was shown in the Salon of 1761, and it was the only model meant specifically for a biscuit that he ever entered in a public exhibition.

The Bather with a Sponge is interesting for a somewhat different reason. Its conception is in deliberate contrast to that of the early Bather: the biscuit Bather is not seen stepping into the water but is drying herself after her bath, and instead of showing the stylistic elements of *lucidity Louis XV*, displays unmistakable marks of Classicism. Gracefully standing with the weight resting on the right foot, the head framed by one arm and the other brought to the shoulder, the figure follows a well-known Classical stance that is often represented in antique statues, as well as in later Classicizing works, such as Jean Goujon's Nymph from the *Fountain of the Innocents* (Fig. 58). In comparison to the earlier Bather, the drapery is no longer crumpled, and the anatomical structure expresses more emphatically the pressure of the body on the ground. *The Bather with a Sponge* retains a suggestion of sensuous coquettishness, but the general feeling of the figure is that of simplicity and logic, which chronologically coincides with Falconet's growing awareness of the "Classical problem."

Like the *Little Girl* and *The Bather with a Sponge*, many biscuits can offer further insight into Falconet's overlapping trends. Ordered in a chronological sequence, these biscuits — some of them, like *Erigone* (Fig. 53), reproducing the sculptor's lost marble statues — can fill a number of stylistic gaps and open a wider perspective on a surprisingly complex evolution. They demonstrate, for instance, that one cannot assume *a priori* a progressive decline of Rococo in Falconet's art. Because of the conservative taste that seems to have prevailed in the commercial requirements of Sèvres, the Rococo style was not allowed to erode. In many cases late biscuits, such as *The Fairy Urgèle* (1766; Fig. 54), are certainly conceived in a more anecdotal manner, but they are not less Rococo than earlier examples, such as *Fishing* (1758; Fig. 59). It appears that Falconet worked simultaneously in Classical and Rococo modes and was practicing both the very year he left for Russia.

In a number of biscuits, for instance in the already mentioned *Magic Lantern* and *Wafers Lottery*, or in *The Meat Cakes* (1759; Fig. 60), Falconet playfully recorded the activities, the customs, and the games of eighteenth-century everyday life. In many others the artist echoed the fashion of certain literary subjects and popular plays. *The Given Kiss* and *The Returned Kiss* (Figs. 61, 62; both 1765), for instance, are derived from La Fontaine, and *The Fairy Urgèle* from Voltaire. Here, as in many others, the themes of the biscuits were directly inspired by the operas of Favart or the productions of the *Théâtre de la Foire*, which often reinterpreted well-known literary themes.

The interest of these biscuits transcends the fragmentary historical information they may contain. Falconet's biscuits are no more merely documents than they are stylistic symptoms or nostalgia-filled bibelots. Their role is similar to that of Graeco-Roman terra-cottas and Tanagra figurines. Despite their smallness, their unpretentiousness, and their fragility, they represent a most significant sculptural fact. Despite their commercial implication, they unquestionably are a major part of Falconet's contribution to art history. Because of their popularity and their diffusion throughout Europe, Sèvres biscuits constituted an overwhelmingly powerful influence. The eighteenth-century "French style," spread by French porcelain, was fated to be the style of Falconet.

The spread of a style through a multiplication of questionable attributions can easily warp the historical image of an artist. This truism is not called forth by the Sèvres biscuits, but by the vexing problem raised by a multitude of small marble statues that are ascribed to Falconet on the strength of unverified tradition. One must realize that — with one significant exception — there is no reason to think that any of these charming statuettes was ever exhibited in the Salons of the eighteenth century, was ever mentioned in the eighteenth-century listings of Falconet's works, or was ever associated with his name in any eighteenth-century sale or critical writing.

The intriguing thing is that many of these small pieces of sculpture belong to easily recognizable categories. In each category the statuettes closely repeat one another, seeming to derive from a single prototype. If one believes that these prototypes were created by Falconet, one must conclude that they remained in obscurity because of some unexplained confusion or because of the sculptor's own decision to remain anonymous.

The first explanation might be plausible in the case of the often repeated type (Figs. 63, 64) of an unusually beautiful nude female figure seated in an attitude reminiscent of the sixteenth-century Diana of Anet. Bringing to mind the rounded, graceful movement of a ballerina, the figure is holding the folds of a rose-filled drapery with one hand, and lifting a rose-filled quiver with the other. Most probably she can be identified as Flora — Flora gathering roses, the symbols of pleasure, from Cupid's quiver. Falconet exhibited two versions of *Flora* in the Salon, the first in 1750, the second in 1753. Since it is known that the latter was a figure holding a garland of flowers, rather than a quiver, it may be conjectured that the theme of "Flora with the Quiver of Roses" was based on the model shown in 1750. From the point of view of attribution, it is important to note that the proportions of this small figure of Flora, the facial expression, the coiffure, and the treatment of the hands unmistakably recall the delicate feminine type that recurs from the early *Bather* (Fig. 20) through the *Winter* (Figs. 39-42). The clarity of forms and the superbly poised and energetic composition, attuned to the oval shape of the base, are directly reminiscent of Falconet's *lucidity Louis XV*. The original statue, executed in stone, is lost, but the lasting popularity of *Flora with the Quiver of Roses* is demonstrated by the great number and the high quality of small marble replicas (averaging 12 inches in height), some of which can be seen in the Hermitage Museum, the Cognac-Jay Museum, and the Walters Art Gallery (Figs. 63-66).

One finds oneself on far more uncertain grounds in considering the host of other statuettes. One cannot indefinitely invoke unexplainable confusion, and it is difficult to believe that Falconet would have chosen to remain secretive in every case. Attempts at attribution are further frustrated by the varying quality of execution and by the stylistic diversity that characterize these small marble works. Among the most attractive examples, one notes the groups organized around the themes of *The Bather with a Towel*, *Venus and Cupid*, and *Love Crowned by Fidelity*. Generally, with these groups, the traditional attribution to Falconet is maintained because of a detail, such as a facial expression or a gesture, or, less specifically, because of what might be called a "Falconet feeling."

The Bather with a Towel continues a well-known series of representations of women posed in the attitude of the Classical *Thorn Puller*, enacting a variety of biblical, mythological, and genre scenes that can explain an after-the-bath episode. A comparison of three instances of *The Bather with a Towel* gives a good idea of the variety of styles that characterizes this group (average size 11 inches). The surprisingly naturalistic work of Lons-le-Saunier (Figs. 67, 68) suggests an attempt to give to *The Bather* the features of a rather mature Madame de Pompadour. In contrast, the statuette of the Cognac-Jay Museum (Fig. 69) shows some indications of a Classical feeling. Finally, the delicate, graceful example from Waddesdon Manor (Fig. 70) makes one think of a very good practitioner, familiar with Falconet's style, who endows the master's qualities with a feeling of the precision of an ivory carving.

This sense of precious miniaturizing also prevails in a series of Anacreontic statuettes in which Venus and Cupid are enacting playful mother and son episodes involving nursing, chastising, consoling, etc. Some good examples can be found in the Wallace

Collection, London (Fig. 72), and in a private collection in Paris (Fig. 73) (average size 13 inches). In this series, as in the *The Bather with a Towel*, a comparison of two or more statuettes with an identical subject reveals perceptible stylistic variations. In general, the figures of these little groups tend to be compositionally busier, more stylized, and more archly frolicsome than the figures in Falconet's comparable biscuits, such as *The Little Girl Hiding Cupid's Bow* (Fig. 56).

The theme of *Love Crowned by Fidelity* can be exemplified by the versions in the Victoria and Albert and in the Frick Museums (Fig. 75). Here, the subject is no longer merely playful, and its interpretation brings to mind the almost mystical overtones of Fragonard's late erotic allegories, such as *The Fountain of Love* (1785, Wallace Collection). The carving shows a further degree of miniaturizing stylization, and the composition, seemingly mounted on stilts, soars in obelisk-fashion. This venturesome arrangement and the many jutting projections suggests the possibility of a bronze model for the group. One may remark that *Love Crowned by Fidelity* (approximately 20 inches) is comparable in size to the Walters *Pygmalion* (about $22\frac{1}{2}$ inches), and it is difficult to understand how its prototype, such a distinctive conception, could have remained so completely unnoticed.

In many instances the untested attribution of such statuettes to Falconet is probably a consequence of the undiscriminating enthusiasm — both aesthetic and commercial — aroused in the late nineteenth century by the famous names of the time of Louis XV. However, even if one admits that a great number of the individual pieces are conspicuously questionable, one cannot discard the hypothesis that some of the groups — like the *Flora with the Quiver of Roses* — are based on Falconet's lost or unrecorded models. In the absence of documentation, it is impossible to come to a final conclusion for the other groups. Very likely the original idea of the prototype was initiated in the circle of Falconet's close associates at Sèvres. Deeply involved in the sculptor's ceramic activities, they acquired the habit of visualizing and imitating his works in a stylized, over-dainty, miniature manner, exemplified in some of the biscuits executed during the 1770's by Le Riche and Boizot.

In order to avoid another source of blurring of the sculptor's image, it would be prudent, in the scope of this book, to abstain from the hazardous game of attributions in the areas of decorative bronzes, silversmith work, and furniture design. It is known that Falconet, like many other eighteenth-century artists, earned considerable sums by providing models for specialists in some of these crafts. There are many tentative attributions, some of them most tempting, such as the beautiful bronze clock in the Besançon Museum (Fig. 71), but the documentation is practically nonexistent. Evidently Falconet did not care to stress this side of his activities. There is an important exception: Gabriel de Saint-Aubin left a tiny sketch (Fig. 74) representing two plaster models (now lost) of silver chandeliers exhibited by Falconet in the Salon of 1761. These chandeliers, which were to be executed by the famous silversmith François-Thomas Germain for a "foreign court," were much admired by the Salon critics for the classical character of their figures.

V

The Drama of Saint-Roch

In the history of sculpture, the church of Saint-Roch is the church of Falconet. It is known that the sculptor worked in at least three other Parisian churches: Saint-Laurent, Saint-André-des-Arts, and the Invalides. However, almost nothing is known about these works, with the exception of the model for a large marble statue of Saint Ambrose (projected for the Invalides, completed by Lemoyne, and lost during the Revolution); the model is recorded in Saint-Aubin's drawing of the Salon of 1765 (Fig. 33). In any case, there is no doubt that the major portion of Falconet's ecclesiastical commissions was related to Saint-Roch, and today it is the only church that still preserves some of his sculpture.

In 1753, Falconet designed for Saint-Roch the tomb of Louise-Elisabeth La Live de Jully, the wife of one of his most faithful patrons, who had died the previous year. The tomb suffered almost total destruction during the Revolution, but its general appearance is known from a contemporary drawing in the Musée Carnavalet (Fig. 76). The effigy of the deceased appears, above the sarcophagus, in an oval medallion that is still preserved in the church (Fig. 77). The sarcophagus, bearing a bronze relief representing *Time Harvesting a Rose at Dawn*, is supported by two brackets, decorated with triglyphs and garlands, which frame the epitaph. On the top of the sarcophagus is a mourning *putto* (wingless angel or wingless Cupid?) leaning on an urn and holding a torch upside down. The sarcophagus is linked to the effigy medallion by a garland of flowers and by the vapor emitted from two incense-burning vases on either side of the *putto*.

This iconographic scheme is obviously very far from the drama of Pigalle's celebrated declamatory mausoleum of Maurice de Saxe, which was begun the same year (Saint-Thomas, Strasbourg), and it might appear that Falconet was content merely to borrow from the standard architectural and allegorical vocabulary of early eighteenth-century wall tombs. The unpretentiousness of his conception is not surprising, for the tomb of a beautiful woman dead at twenty-five called for an elegy rather than an epic poem, and the sculptor chose to stress simplicity and refinement of proportions. He relied on a homespun type of imagery, which was probably suggested to him by his patron, and he allowed himself no more than a touch of late Baroque theatricality in the marble-carved vapor rising toward the medallion, illusionistically enveloping the floral garland. Deliberately shrinking from ostentatiousness, the sculptor succeeded in giving his monument the intimacy of private sorrow and the quiet elegance of an eighteenth-century typographical tail-piece.

The year of this tomb's completion, Falconet was given the commission for the extensive renovations enthusiastically planned for Saint-Roch by its new vicar, the Abbé Jean-Baptiste Marduel. This award was the result of a competition organized after the rejection of an earlier project, submitted by Servandoni, the famous architect of the façade of Saint-Sulpice, because it failed to comply with the wishes of Marduel.

The plan of Saint-Roch, drawn in the seventeenth century by Jacques Lemercier, included beyond the crossing a sequence of oval chapels which followed the axis of the central nave (Fig. 78). Realizing the dramatic possibilities of this disposition, the Abbé Marduel hoped to bring forth a unified view of the succession of chapels, each one of them preserving its religious and aesthetic significance yet opening into the others. The flowing sequence of spatial units was to include the crossing, the choir, the chapel of the Virgin, the chapel of the Communion, and the chapel of the Calvary (added in 1754 to the north end of the church). Working in collaboration with the architect Etienne-Louis Boullée, the painter Jean-Baptiste-Marie Pierre, and several other artists, Falconet was entrusted with the direction of the project. One must keep in mind that he was expected to act as "stage manager" as well as sculptor. In both capacities he had to listen to Marduel and take into account the limitation of the resources at his disposal.

Falconet's activity at Saint-Roch encompassed a period of approximately seven years (1753-1760). In the absence of any clear chronology of his various contributions to Marduel's project, one can best discuss them in the order in which they were to appear to an eighteenth-century visitor progressing from the crossing toward the north end.

For orientation, a good starting point is provided by Charles Norry's drawing (ca. 1787) of the interior of Saint-Roch (Fig. 79). At the far left corner of the crossing (recognizable by its hemispherical dome), just before the entrance to the choir, Falconet placed his statue of *Christ in Agony in the Garden of Olives*. This figure, set against a pillar, balanced the *Saint-Roch* of Guillaume Coustou, which was similarly situated on the right of the crossing. Both works were erected on blue marble altars decorated with urns and gilded reliefs.

In his statue of *Christ* (Figs. 80, 81), Falconet altered the accepted iconography of the subject. His figure is detached from the traditional representation of *Christ in the Garden of Olives*, which normally includes the sleeping Apostles and the vision of the Angel. Such an isolated image of *Christ in Agony* is very seldom encountered in art. Curiously, Falconet's *Christ* is conceived in the manner of some single figures of the late Middle Ages, such as the *Man of Sorrows* and the *Virgin of Pity*, in which the expression of pathos is intensified through a suggestion of introspection, conveyed by loneliness. This feeling of introspection is also intimated by the instruments of the Passion (nails and crown of thorns) lying at Christ's feet, attributes of the inner vision of his agony. This iconographical concept was perhaps suggested by the Abbé Marduel to mark the first station of the Way of the Cross, which culminates in the chapel of the Calvary.

After being moved to and fro during the Revolutionary period, Falconet's *Christ in Agony*, deprived of its blue marble altar, was returned to its original location in Saint-Roch, where it can be seen today. The large stone statue (about 6 feet) brings directly to mind the ecstatic swooning and suffering of Bernini's *Saint Teresa*, in the Cornaro Chapel (Fig. 83) — a work greatly admired by Falconet. With his head thrown sideways and his limp, hanging arms, the *Christ in Agony* almost duplicates the pantomime of Bernini's figure. It is difficult to agree with Diderot, who found in the *Christ* the same lack of unity as in the *Milo of Crotona*, complaining that the upper part of the statue expressed agony while its lower part expressed rest. Yet one must admit that Falconet's *Christ in Agony* lacks the bravura and the flesh and blood vigor of Bernini's saints. His strangely awkward and self-conscious languidness, and his complicated but somewhat flattened drapery are reminiscent of some earlier French variations on Berninesque ecstasy, such as Jean Restout's painting of *The Death of Saint Scholastica* (1730; Fig. 82). Whatever its exact sources, it is obvious that Falconet's figure of *Christ* is far more Baroque than his *Cupid* or his *Bather*, and it is hard to believe that these two statues appeared in the Salon of 1757 alongside the terra-cotta model of the *Christ!* During the eighteenth century, ecclesiastical art remained deeply Baroque, and certain ecclesiastical subjects seemed to carry on their own built-in stylistic tradition, regardless of the changes which might have been occurring in the other works of a given artist.

Thus, the Baroque spirit also prevailed, not unexpectedly, in Falconet's decoration of the chapel of the Virgin. This gigantic sculptural composition unfolded behind the high altar, on the level of the arch separating the chapel of the Virgin from the chapel of the Communion (Fig. 85). The magnificent white-and-gold ensemble, one of the landmarks of Saint-Roch, showed the two figures of the Annunciation, Mary and Gabriel, flanked by the prophets David and Isaiah, and united from above by the clouds of a celestial Glory. This iconographic program, enriched on the vault by Pierre's painting of *The Assumption of the Virgin*, is typically Baroque; the distant echoes of medieval tradition, surviving in the introduction of the two Old Testament prophets who foretold the Incarnation, are not uncommon in Baroque iconography.

The arresting effect of Falconet's decoration is suggested by its measurement: approximately 9 feet for each one of the figures of the Annunciation, 8 feet for the prophets, and a total area of 55×33 feet for the Glory. Of this ensemble, only the Glory escaped, almost unscathed, from Revolutionary vandalism, and for the rest one is frustratingly limited to eighteenth-century secondary material.

Little can be said about the kneeling figure of the Virgin, which is barely visible in a diminitive detail of Norry's drawing. The terra-cotta model of the statue was exhibited in the Salon of 1755, where it was praised for its simple grace and for the good taste and the lightness of the drapery. The figure of Gabriel, pointing to the Glory, is known from the same drawing by Norry as well as from an engraving that Pierre-Etienne Falconet executed for Diderot's *Encyclopedia*, showing the arrival of the angel at Saint-Roch in 1758 (Fig. 84). The critics admired the feeling of suppleness and weightlessness conveyed by the statue despite its huge marble mass. The figures of David and Isaiah are only faintly discernible in Norry's drawing. David was noted because of his Oriental garb, and Isaiah because of his austere but noble drapery; both prophets attracted attention because they were cast in lead and gilded. Diderot in his 1760 description of Saint-Roch, published by Grimm, finds that the figures of Mary and Gabriel have a somewhat rustic character; he greatly admires the austere looks of Isaiah, but notes that David looks like a "fat wagoner." Curiously enough, Falconet himself is reported to have said that his Isaiah looked like a "fat cook."

There is little doubt that the Glory of Saint-Roch — the largest example of its kind in France — was the chief attraction of Falconet's ensemble (Fig. 86). It had been obviously inspired by Bernini's Glory of Saint Peter (Fig. 87). Yet because of the relatively smaller proportions of the church of Saint-Roch, Falconet's Glory seems to be larger than Bernini's. Because of its simpler design — including more billowy clouds and darting shafts of light and fewer cherubs — it also seems to be what one might call, rather improperly, "more realistic" than its famous seventeenth-century counterpart. Paradoxically, it was Falconet's purported lack of illusion and interference with the architecture of the church that was the primary source of the controversy embroiling him with de la Garde, the librarian of Madame de Pompadour. This controversy inspired a series of heated exchanges and a caricature by Cochin (1763) showing *Phylakei* (de la Garde) "writing against the Glory of Monsieur Falconet, which he does not see, or sees only through a broken visual ray" (Fig. 88). For his part, Falconet, in *L'Observateur littéraire* of October 1759, had already proudly proclaimed that his intention was to follow the illustrious example of Bernini, in every respect. According to him, the very existence of Bernini's Glory provided a victorious retort to all disparaging remarks, including the criticism of his superimposition of the rays of the Glory over the pilasters of the church.

Today nobody would challenge Falconet's right to a marble Glory — realistic or not — nor his right to design a Glory that interferes with the geometrical integrity of the pilasters of the church. Compositionally, his Glory was indispensable to bring unity to a sculptural ensemble divided by the opening of a huge arch: the pattern of clouds, rays, and cherubs initiated a dynamic figure eight which completed itself, on ground level, in the group of the Annunciation.

Above all, the joyful white-and-gold symphony of Falconet's Glory represented an impressive attempt to revitalize the dramatic possibilities of the Baroque vocabulary. The same intention was expressed in a far more somber mode in the chapel of the Calvary, which, framed by the arch of the chapel of the Virgin, appeared in the distance between the white marble figures of Mary and Gabriel. A painting attributable to Pierre-Antoine De Machy (*ca.* 1770), long overlooked until its recent location by the author in the Museum of Pau, offers important new information about Falconet's decoration of this chapel, which was destroyed during the nineteenth century. The documentary interest of this *View of the Chapel of the Calvary* (Figs. 89, 90) is enhanced by its large size (about 50 × 38 inches), by the well-known literalism of De Machy's architectural renditions, and by the fact that this painter was personally involved in the decoration of the chapel.

The study of the chapel of the Calvary can be based on the evidence of De Machy's painting, verified by the description — a kind of press release — which was published in the *Mercure de France* of December 1760, before the official opening of the newly decorated chapels. In the back of the chapel was a group composed of the crucified Christ and the kneeling Mary Magdalen. Framed by the arch-like opening of a stony grotto bordered with vegetation, these two statues were placed against a painting (by De Machy) of a cloudy sky, which seemed to continue the space of the three-dimensional grotto. Immediately in front of this group, on the top of a craggy elevation formed by a mass of boulders (held together with metallic clamps), were two reclining Roman guards, a huge coiling serpent which seemed to be hissing at the cross, a broken tree, and tufts of vegetation. Below, in a cave-like recess, stood a marble altar (designed by Boullée), with two incense-burning urns placed on either side of a truncated bronze column supporting the instruments of the Passion. To have a clearer idea of this ensemble, one must remember that there was a light source behind the opening of the grotto that gave the illusion of light coming from the painted landscape. It is also important to observe that this sculptural arrangement was anything but black and white. In addition to the blue marble altar, the gilded bronze column, and the blue-greens and the yellow-ochers of the painted sky, the visitor to the chapel saw a number of "naturally" tinted details, such as the orange-gray tree stump, the bluish serpent, and the pale green grass.

By leaving his figures in monochrome (marble or stone painted in imitation of marble), Falconet avoided the dangers of the dubious illusionism of a *tableau vivant*, such as the famous fifteenth-century *Way of the Cross* in Varallo. Yet these figures are given comparatively little attention: Mary Magdalen belongs to the seventeenth- and eighteenth-century ecclesiastical repertory, and the group of the Roman soldiers makes one think of two fishermen in disguise transferred to the chapel from a painting of Joseph Vernet. Probably for the sake of economy (Marduel's finances were apparently running short), Falconet did not sculpt his own figure of the crucified Christ but simply borrowed a statue by the seventeenth-century sculptor Michel Anguier, which was already at Saint-Roch.

Falconet's iconography is more interesting for its staging than for its content. With its dramatically stage-managed source of light, tragic sky, broken tree, and superimposed grottoes, the naturalistically colored decoration of the chapel probably resembled a typical bit of rocky shore in a *Shipwreck* by Vernet or the scenery De Machy painted for Gluck's opera, *Orpheus*. The critics praised the pathos of Falconet's conception, except Diderot, who felt that the setting was too small and too light. Today these elements are difficult to judge. Whatever its true effectiveness, it is certain that in its spirit, Falconet's decoration falls historically somewhere between the picturesqueness of the Baroque stage and the "sublimity" of the Romantic landscape. In a general manner, such an effect will be revived in 1827 in Georges-Philippe Clésinger's *Grotte de Sainte Madeleine* in the church of Mary Magdalen in Besançon.

The whole program of Saint-Roch must be visualized in terms of a theatrical perspective. Introduced by the *Christ in Agony*, it reveals a succession of altars and arches, with a major accent on the Glory and the *Annunciation* and a final climax in the somber, panorama-like chapel of the Calvary. Falconet demonstrated at Saint-Roch the interest in dramatic staging that will reach its greatest development in his statue of Peter the Great.

VI

The Problem of Portraits,
Late Allegory, and the Epic
of The Bronze Horseman

FALCONET'S most prestigious commission, the equestrian statue of the Russian czar Peter I — "Peter the Great" — was essentially an allegorical portrait. Ironically, after accomplishments in so many different areas of his profession, the sculptor was given a once-in-a-lifetime opportunity to reach hitherto unequaled heights in the type of work he was least prepared to undertake. All his life he had been averse to portraiture — he nursed for it something akin to a phobia — and he had had a very limited and frustrating experience in the art of official allegory.

These factors deserve some consideration. There are only four existing portraits attributable to Falconet prior to *Peter the Great:* the terra-cotta bust of Dr. Camille Falconet at the age of seventy-six (1747; Fig. 91); the marble medallion of Madame La Live de Jully on her tomb at Saint-Roch (1753; Fig. 77); the allegorical biscuit of Madame de Pompadour as *Friendship* (1755; Figs. 94, 95); and the marble bust of Dr. Camille Falconet at the age of eighty-nine (1760; Fig. 93).

The biscuit and the medallion do not require a lengthy discussion. The biscuit of *Friendship* — the earliest of Falconet's *Friendships* (see chapter III) — was specifically described in the Sale Register of Sèvres as a portrait of Madame de Pompadour. However, this allegorical biscuit can be considered as an individualized likeness only by stretching one's imagination, for it shows little beyond the highly stylized elegance and idealization of the period. The effigy of Madame La Live de Jully, which was probably done after Cochin's engraving of a drawing by the subject's husband, shows a delicate but strongly delineated profile. In introducing some naturalistic touches, such as the puffy eyes and the protruding upper lip, the sculptor succeeded in giving a measure of individual life to an otherwise stereotyped face. It is a charming work, but it recalls scores of similar eighteenth-century profiles with upturned noses.

It is only in the two busts of his namesake, Dr. Camille Falconet, that one can really study Falconet as a portrait sculptor. A comparison of these two works immediately shows that the earlier terra-cotta (in Lyons) is more momentary, livelier, and warmer than the marble (in Angers), in which the eyes seem to be more sunken, the mouth more open, and the wrinkles deeper. However, if one takes into account the contrast produced by the majestic wig of the early representation and the baldness of the later one, and if one considers the unavoidable technical differences that separate a terra-cotta and a marble, it appears that the two conceptions are extremely similar. Significantly, Falconet himself mentions only one bust of Dr. Falconet, one in marble — a fact possibly suggesting that he considered the early terra-cotta merely as a study for the final marble bust. This interpretation seems to be verified by the identical treatment of the details of the clothes, as well as by the identical Greek inscription appearing on the back of both statues: "One of the two namesakes represented the other. The younger did the older" (Fig. 92).

Thus, it is probable that the sculptor, in the process of belatedly translating his terra-cotta sketch into the final marble form (after thirteen years), made some changes that reflected the aging of his model. In the later conception, the emergence of the intellectual life, purified, as it were, by the physical decrepitude of old age — an idea which will be applied to Voltaire both by Pigalle (1776) and by Houdon (1778) — is underlined by the removal of the ornamental wig. While the brilliant, impressionistic spontaneity of the early bust continues the tradition of Lemoyne's portraiture, the later marble bust shows an extraordinary combination of minute naturalism and stylization. It is difficult to imagine a more medically accurate rendition of senility. Yet at close range the smallest details reveal a sense of stylization, from the almost ornamental curls of the sparse hair to the two comma-like incisions catching the light in the pupil of each eye. There is a strange confrontation between the closely, almost anatomically, observed physical fact and an apparent need to record it in a studiously defined handwriting. In this bust, the effortlessly stylized naturalism of Bernini's Baroque tradition has grown into a painstaking technique in which every chisel mark suggests a hard-won battle.

Camille Falconet, a distant relative of the sculptor, was known as the consulting physician of the king as well as an enthusiastic bibliophile. In undertaking his bust, the artist was pointing to a flattering kinship and repaying the kindness of this famous man of science and letters, who opened his library to the sculptor and took pleasure in his conversation. The enormous success enjoyed by *Dr. Falconet* in the Salon of 1761, where it was praised for its uncanny likeness, realism, and expressiveness, did nothing to encourage the sculptor to pursue similar tasks. Thus, in 1763, incongruously claiming lack of competence, he declined the important official commission of a full-length statue of Madame Adelaïde, one of the king's daughters. Somewhat later, it is true, he executed a marble bust of his friend Diderot. However, upon comparing it to the marble *Diderot* carved by Mademoiselle Collot, he dramatically acknowledged his inferiority by breaking his own bust to pieces with a hammer.

In official allegory, Falconet's apparent lack of achievement was a consequence of adverse circumstances rather than a question of phobia. It has already been seen how much he disliked the group of *France Embracing the Bust of Louis XV* (see Chap. II). At the time he was asking the Marquis de Marigny to be excused from this uninspiring project on which he had been erratically toiling under the guidance of Charles Coypel, he began to work on two allegorical marble statues commissioned by the Duke Charles Eugene of Württemberg: the *Sovereignty of Princess* and the *Glory of Princes* (1761). Falconet started the carving when he had received half of the 22,000 *livres* agreed upon for the commission, but, showing a businessman's pragmatism, he did not want to deliver or even to finish the statues before the complete payment of the stipulated sum. Because of the Duke's financial difficulties, the two statues remained in the sculptor's studio until his departure for Russia. Eventually the unfinished statues were purchased by Catherine II (in 1766), and they were probably completed, in Saint Petersburg, about this time.

Despite their large size ($7\frac{1}{2}$ feet), these two allegories remained so completely unnoticed in Russia that it is impossible to say when they disappeared. Extremely little is known about them. In 1766, writing to Betzki about Falconet's coming to Russia, Diderot perfunctorily mentions that the figure of *Sovereignty* was leaning on fasces and that *Glory* was placing a garland around a medallion — which, he suggests, could offer a good place for the image of the Empress. Diderot's succinct description of Falconet's *Glory* can be applied to a statue titled *The Glory of Catherine II* in the Jacquemart-André Museum (Fig. 96). One can agree with Réau that this small statue (39 inches) can plausibly be identified as a later and smaller version of the original allegory. Evidently derived from the corresponding emblem of Ripa's *Iconologia*, the Jacquemart-André *Glory* is holding on a column a medallion bearing the helmeted and laureled profile of Catherine II and is placing a garland of flowers around it. This statue does not correspond to any of Falconet's previously discussed stylistic trends. Some details (for instance, the flowers) are roughly carved, and the extremely intricate drapery stylistically contradicts the highly idealized and simplified face of the figure. It is possible, naturally, that such inconsistencies could be explained by a later hand — the statue could have been completed or reworked by a Russian sculptor — but whatever the case, the dullness of *Glory's* iconography clearly indicates that Falconet was not particularly inspired by this type of official imagery.

When the sculptor accepted the commission of the equestrian bronze statue of Peter the Great, he undoubtedly took into account his distaste for portraiture and his lack of interest in official allegory. But in addition, he was forced to consider the disturbing fact that he had never sculpted a horse or cast a bronze statue. These problems had to be overcome, but it was no longer merely a question of patience, willpower, or routine professional ambition. For Falconet, the Russian commission was an unhoped-for call to greatness. Everything that had happened to him before appeared insignificant and mediocre. At the time he was turning fifty, he was transfixed by the bolt of lightning that kindled all his artistic resources and energies. Old frustrations and new obstacles were to be subordinated to the vital opportunity of manifesting whatever genius he could muster.

The first idea of the project that brought Falconet to Russia had originated in the lifetime of Peter the Great; but the equestrian monument begun during the czar's reign by the Italian sculptor Carlo Bartolomeo Rastrelli could not be completed before Peter's death (1725). For political reasons, his successors, Catherine I, Peter II, and Anna Ivanovna, showed no inclination to support the project, and it remained dormant until Peter the

Great's daughter, Elizabeth, became Empress in 1741. However, Rastrelli died almost immediately, in 1744; and his statue, finally cast in 1761 by Alessandro Martelli, was finished far too late to be set up before the end of Elizabeth's reign (1762). The project was revived a second time by Catherine II. For the new Empress — who was foreign-born and who acceded to the throne in the midst of suspicious circumstances surrounding the murder of her husband, Peter III — the monument of Peter the Great meant much more than a glorification of a famous predecessor. For her, such a monument was endowed with far-reaching political significance. It symbolized the legitimacy of her position by dramatizing her allegiance to the great task undertaken by the most famous and the most revered of all the Russian czars.

Such a personal aim could hardly be fulfilled by an ancient statue ordered by another monarch. After some deliberation, Catherine II decided on a completely new monument and a completely new conception. The final rejection of Rastrelli's statue, in 1764, was the signal for a variety of new proposals. Most of them expounded ponderous allegories in the spirit of Baroque iconology. For example, Betzki, the official administrator of the project, wanted to encumber the monument with an incredible apparatus of allegories, trophies, reliefs, and lengthy Greek and Latin inscriptions carefully spelling out every single achievement of Peter the Great's reign. Diderot, who always loved to give advice to artists, joined the chorus of idea-givers; he saw the monument as a huge fountain, with the figure of Peter dominating the allegorical personification of People's Love, the Nation, and Barbarism.

Falconet turned a deaf ear to all the proposals. In fact, he had already found the essential idea for his statue while he was still in Paris. Caught in a sketch jotted down during one of his visits to Diderot, this idea was further defined in a three-dimensional wax model before his departure for Russia, and was later approved by the Empress in Saint Petersburg. Strengthened by the knowledge of her support — she had advised him to be guided by his "stubbornness" — he declared to Diderot that his monument would be simple. In its general lines, Falconet's conception is indeed heroically simple: Peter the Great is represented on a rearing horse, at the top of a rocky elevation — there is no *overt* symbolical detail of any kind, with the exception of a serpent winding behind the horse (Fig. 98).

In this conception, Falconet departed from the main tradition of equestrian monuments, which took its source in the Roman statue of Marcus Aurelius, in the Capitoline square (Fig. 99). This tradition was based on the image of a triumphant horseman mounted on a powerful steed, majestically advancing at a walking pace on the flat surface of a geometrically shaped pedestal. Exemplified during the Italian Renaissance by Donatello's *Gattamelata* (Padua) and Verrocchio's *Colleoni* (Venice), this type of equestrian representation culminated in France in Girardon's famous statue of Louis XIV, which stood in the Place Vendôme, in Paris (Fig. 101). In the eighteenth century, the same basic type inspired Saly's *Frederick V* (Copenhagen), Bouchardon's statue of Louis XV in the Place Louis XV, in Paris, and a statue of the same king by Lemoyne, at Bordeaux (Fig. 2).

Falconet's rejection of the Marcus Aurelius type did not mean that he began with a tabula rasa and that he proceeded to re-invent every element of the equestrian image. Some aspects of his conception are not without precedents. The theme of the rider on a rearing horse, for instance, is often used in Classical reliefs; later it appears in Bernini's ill-fated statue of Louis XIV (Fig. 102) (renamed *Marcus Curtius*, at Versailles), and it recurs, in a series of eighteenth-century bronze statuettes (variously attributed to Desjardins and to Guillaume de Groff) representing Louis XIV (Fig. 100) and other European rulers. This concept of the ruler on a rearing horse, evolved from the emblem of the victorious Caesar, shows a tendency toward formality, and most often in such images the act of rearing varies from a suggestion of formalized gallop to that of a riding-school curvet.

In placing Peter the Great's rearing horse on the edge of a rocky elevation, Falconet gave to the old theme an unprecedented dramatic context. It is impossible, of course, to retrace the genesis of Falconet's creative process. Thus one cannot say whether this new concept was originally inspired only by a desire for a picturesque effect, such as Bernini achieved in the *Fountain of the Four Rivers* (Piazza Navona, Rome), or by an attempt to bring in the note of awesomeness he had previously introduced in the rocky landscaping of the chapel of the Calvary. Nevertheless, it is certain that almost from the beginning the sculptor gave his imagery an inner symbolic meaning.

The symbolism of *Peter the Great* must be visualized in its proper frame of reference. The earlier experience of *France Embracing the Bust of Louis XV* and of the *Glory of Princes* had taught Falconet the danger of allegorical excesses. He did not want to banish allegory entirely from art, but he came to the conclusion, as he states in the *Récapitulation* of his *Observations sur la statue de Marc-Aurèle*, that a statue should be able to speak for itself and that allegory should not be superimposed on its subject as a "superfluous sign." Thus, in *Peter the Great*, the sculptor's symbolism is functionally integrated with the subject. In answer to Diderot's allegorical suggestions for his statue (1766), the artist proclaimed: "My hero is self-sufficient; he is his own subject and his own attribute." Beyond any doubt, the sculptor did a good amount of reading on the life of Peter the Great. In a letter to Diderot, published twice (1770 and 1781), Falconet admits that his conception of the czar came to coincide with that of Voltaire, referring to a group of letters of Voltaire's related to his projected *History of Russia Under the Reign of Peter the Great*. In one of these letters (to Count Shuvaloff, July 1759), the writer states that this czar deserved a special gratitude from later generations, for, while all monarchs led negociations, besieged cities, and fought wars, he was the only ruler to have reformed the ways of life of his empire and to have laid the foundations of its arts, its fleet, and its trade. This was the idea that was to govern the statue of Falconet, since he believed that a sculptor, by the nature of his art, is compelled to limit himself to one aspect only of a great man's character, and that he should select this aspect to correspond to the one virtue that contributed most to the happiness of humanity. Thus, Falconet shows Peter the Great not as a conqueror, but as a benevolent reformer and legislator; the monarch of the *philosophes* and the benefactor of the new Russia.

In his writings, Falconet repeatedly explained the meaning of the various aspects of his statue. Instead of the traditional pseudo-Roman martial attire, the czar is given a "heroic" but nondescript garb which, according to the sculptor, belongs to "men of all times." The sculptor acknowledges the fact that this garb recalls the shirt worn by Volga boatmen, and one can note an additional, distinctly Russian, touch in the wolf skin used as the monarch's saddle — the nature of this fur is clearly identifiable in a small bronze statuette of the monument, in a private Dutch collection (Fig. 104). The czar protectively extends his fatherly hand over his kingdom (his famous victory of Poltava is alluded to, in a most indirect way, only by his laurels and his sword). He has reached the summit of the rocky elevation that symbolizes the difficulties he has overcome. Crushing under its hooves the serpent of envy in the course of its rapid upward gallop, the czar's horse, suddenly restrained by its master's iron hand, is rearing on the brink of the cliff. In the same heroic vein, Falconet, rejecting the pedantry of the texts suggested for the monument, recaptured the spirit of the epigraphic laconism of Antiquity in an inscription (appearing both in Russian and in Latin) which pithily expresses the Empress's political intention:

TO PETER I
CATHERINE II

Falconet seems to have been fascinated by the challenge of representing a horse, which was a completely new problem for him. In terms of the increasingly Classically oriented eighteenth century, the horse of an equestrian statue — any equestrian statue — automatically evoked what was thought to be the greatest Classical equine prototype of all times: the horse of Marcus Aurelius. It has already been shown that in the mind of Falconet anything that could be construed as a "Classical problem" stimulated, above all, a spirit of rivalry. In this sense, the problem of Peter the Great's horse fell under the shadow of the "Classical problem," and Falconet rejected a priori the horse of Marcus Aurelius as a model. Colored by bias, this rejection was followed by a detailed condemnation, based on the study of a plaster cast, which was published in his *Observations sur la statue de Marc-Aurèle* (1771). According to Falconet, Marcus Aurelius' horse was not only unsightly because of its bovine head, its ugly thick neck, and, in general, its unpleasant proportions, but it was also objectionable because of its anatomical inadequacies and its unrealistic movement — a real horse, for instance, would never lift its foreleg to a horizontal position.

Falconet's iconoclastic comments (which four years later would inspire Goethe's *Nach Falconet and über Falconet*) were not overlooked by the lovers of Classical art, who proceeded to ridicule him for criticizing a Roman masterpiece he had never seen. While smarting under their barbs for describing a famous Classical statue as a bad horse, he was constantly spurred on by Diderot's letters to produce a "sublime" one. Disregarding celebrated models, the sculptor decided to work directly from nature. He began to study a variety of beautiful horses he selected in the stables of the Empress and of Count Orloff, her favorite. To help the artist, an equerry was asked to ride a horse at full gallop, again and again, on the top of an artificial hillock (specially built for this purpose), where he suddenly stopped to cause the rearing of the animal. After innumerable drawings and terra-cotta sketches recording his observations of the animal from every angle and his analysis of the galloping motion, the play of muscles, and the resulting tension of the skin, Falconet was ready to "invent" his horse. This approach, which recalls Leonardo and Barye, was guided by a sense of aesthetic unity as much as by a need for scientific investigation. Such union of creative imagination and scrupulousness was very uncommon in the eighteenth century, and as a result, Peter the Great's horse is unquestionably the most powerfully original and realistic representation of this animal of the period (Fig. 105). Freeing itself from Baroque stylization, Falconet's passionate horse anticipates the concept of David's *Bonaparte Crossing the Alps* (Versailles) and the fiery naturalism of Géricault and Delacroix.

In comparison with his horse, Falconet's horseman is somewhat anticlimactic. The cavalry general Melissino, who was reputed to have the same height and the same build as Peter the Great, posed for the figure. With the exception of the outstretched hand — a gesture held to have great symbolical significance by Count Orloff — the figure of the czar does not seem to have offered any particular difficulty. Melissino, however, was an accomplished riding master, and this very fact lent to Peter the Great's bearing something of the stiff formality of the manege, unconsciously recorded by the realism-seeking artist.

Naturally, Melissino did not pose for the head of the figure. At the time Falconet was working on his statue, Peter the Great's features were familiar to everybody. Some forty-odd years after the czar's death, his likeness could be studied in many portraits: most reliably, in a life-mask made by Rastrelli in 1723 (Hermitage). Thus, Falconet's problem was not a question of finding documented facts, but of adapting documented facts to the monumental requirements of his project. Yet the sculptor was hypnotized by his strange sense of inadequacy in portraiture, and after three frustrating attempts, he relinquished the task of the head to his pupil, Marie-Anne Collot. Looking at Mademoiselle Collot's head of Peter the Great (Fig. 108), one fails to find the traces of the physiognomical details she usually lavished on her busts. Considering the official purport of the statue, it is not surprising that she found it necessary to temper the awesome reality recorded in Rastrelli's mask. Her czar's idealized, rather puffy face unquestionably conveys aloofness and inner-energy, but it falls short of being the character-revealing, daring, and expressive portrait described by Falconet. Very probably the sculptor — who caused much eyebrow-raising by entrusting to a mere pupil the execution of such an important part of his statue — lent a hand to Mademoiselle Collot in bringing Peter the Great's head into stylistic harmony with the rest of his figure.

The life-size plaster model of the statue, known from a drawing by the Russian painter Anton Losenko (Fig. 106), was exhibited in Falconet's Saint Petersburg studio in May 1770. This model was meant to be faithfully reproduced, through casting, in a huge bronze statue (about 17 feet high). To reduce the weight of the projected statue and also to save expensive metal, Falconet planned to use the traditional "lost wax" casting technique, which produced a hollow bronze shell. The great difficulty presented in casting Peter the Great's monument was the necessity of varying the thickness of the walls of the bronze shell, in order to lighten the front of the statue and to place the greatest possible weight on its rear. Such an uneven shell was indispensable for a secure balance of the monument on its rocky base. Because of the rearing horse, the statue could be given only three points of support: the two hind legs of the horse and the horse's tail linked to the serpent as a buttressing device.

The search for a master-founder capable of undertaking such a complex casting proved to be a major problem. Unable to secure the services of Gor, the famous founder of Bouchardon's *Louis XV*, Falconet hired the Alsatian Benoît Ersman (1772). Ersman was a competent craftsman, and he made all the necessary preparations for the casting. However, his outspoken skepticism about the outcome exasperated Falconet, who finally dismissed him and decided to take personal charge of the casting (1774). The sculptor fully realized the difficulties, for he had had the opportunity to observe the casting of Lemoyne's *Louis XV*. His only important direct previous experience with metal, the making of the two lead prophets of Saint-Roch, was not particularly helpful in working bronze, and five years earlier (in 1769) he had failed in his attempt to cast the small figure of his *Cupid*.

After another — this time successful — experiment in small-scale bronze casting, a copy of the Classical *Thorn Puller* (1774), Falconet undertook his major venture, armed with the published descriptions of the casting of Girardon's *Louis XIV* and of Bouchardon's *Louis XV*. The first casting of *Peter the Great* (1775) was only partially satisfactory. Because of the negligence of one of Falconet's assistants, the fire prepared for the operation was allowed to become so intense that it destroyed the upper part of the mold. Without the presence of mind of Kayloff, the Russian artillery founder attached to Falconet, the statue would have been completely lost. The second attempt (1777), however, aiming at casting the part of the statue damaged by the fire, proved to be a complete success. The separate parts produced by the two successive castings were joined together so skillfully that the seam became totally invisible. The sculptor could claim that he had successfully combined the art of the sculptor and the art of the founder, that his technical mishaps were negligible, and that, in the last regard, his *Peter the Great* was cast all of a piece, like the celebrated equestrian statues of Girardon and of Bouchardon.

The story of the base of *Peter the Great* is a saga in itself. Originally, Falconet planned to erect his statue upon an artificially constructed hillock made up, like the rocky elevation of the Saint-Roch Calvary, of separate stones held together with metallic clamps. Eventually this project was superseded by the idea of a Greek engineer, Carburi-Laskary, who convinced the sculptor, Betzki, and Catherine II that a large single stone would provide a stronger and a more durable support. Since large stones were unavailable in the Saint Petersburg region, an intensive search was undertaken by the Russian Academy of Science, and eventually a rock of the required size was located in a Karelian swamp, about 4 miles from the Gulf of Finland. This gigantic monolith had an auspicious legendary aura. It was called "*Grom-Kamen*," *Thunder-Stone*, because it had been struck by lightning, and it was believed locally that Peter the Great himself had used it several times as an observation point. The transportation of this colossal mass, which weighed three million pounds when it was raised from the swamp, exacted all of Carburi-Laskary's considerable inventiveness. Using ingenious devices, such as copper spheres rolling on wooden rails, and teams of hundreds of mujiks rhythmically pulling cables by the roll of drums, the *Thunder-Stone* was moved to the seacoast. From there, a huge raft tied between two ships brought it to the Neva pier at Saint Petersburg.

The entire *Grom-Kamen* operation took two years (September 1768—September 1770). By order of the Empress, a medal was struck to commemorate its successful completion, and numerous men of letters proceeded to compose narrations and poems comparing the Russian engineering triumph to the building of the pyramids and other grandiose accomplishments of Antiquity. Meanwhile, Falconet — who had had nothing to do with either the selection or the transportation of the celebrated monolith — was being censured for using only a portion of it for the base of his statue (his base was still about 16 feet high!). Obviously, the sculptor was not prepared to equate grandeur with bigness, and he was not likely to allow the *Thunder-Stone* to overshadow the design of his monument. He carved out from the huge granite mass the shape intended for the base in the same spirit he would have carved it from a block of marble. This shape, which has been variously compared to a crouching sphinx and to a rising wave, vitalizes the image of what Falconet called the symbol of the czar's conquered obstacles by echoing the czar's impetuous movement.

Peter the Great was placed on its base by the Russian sculptor Fedor Gordief, who had previously helped Falconet in the finishing stages of the work. Falconet himself, victim of Betzki's scheming and deeply embittered, had left Russia shortly after the completion of the casting (1778). After twelve years of soul-destroying dedication, fate gave Falconet neither the opportunity to erect his statue, nor to attend its inauguration. Commemorated by a second official medal, this inauguration — without the sculptor — was a grandiose assertion of the historical kinship of the reigns of Peter and Catherine, symbolized in the monument. The ceremony was held, in the presence of the Empress, on August 7, 1782, in the immense square of the Senate, with the participation of warships on the Neva river, eight regiments of Guards, and an enormous cheering crowd.

From this time on, the monument became more and more identified as a symbol of Saint Petersburg, rather than as a work of art of a French sculptor. Increasingly russified, *Peter the Great* began to sink deep folkloric roots. For example, the great czar's statue, elevated to the role of the patron saint of the city, was credited with a reassuring appearance in the dream of a Russian officer during Napoleon's advance on Saint Petersburg. In a less benign role, in Pushkin's famous Romantic poem, *The Bronze Horseman*, the statue vengefully pursued a man through the streets of Saint Petersburg, a part recalling that of the *Commendatore's* statue in *Don Giovanni*. Benevolent or ominous, *Peter the Great* came to be popularly visualized as the jealous guardian of the destiny of the city, a kind of awesome palladium.

It is difficult to detach Falconet's statue from the large square — renamed the Square of the Decembrists — where it stands, and from the Neva river to which it seems to be pointing (Fig. 103). Yet, overgrown as it is with Russian myths and memories of Saint Petersburg floods and Saint Petersburg white nights, the formidable *Bronze Horseman* belongs to the history of western art.

Peter the Great occupies a unique position in the evolution of equestrian monuments. What could be construed as its shortcomings — for instance, the somewhat wooden, incongruously garbed figure of the czar — subsides into insignificance in the context of its gigantic silhouette. It is not a mere question of size. The arresting effect of this silhouette is also the result of a powerful ascending diagonal movement which abruptly releases its energy after having reached its apogee. Animated by a different rhythm, the theme of upward élan, culmination, and break is repeated twice: in the bronze horseman, with the horse rearing over emptiness, and in the mountain-like base, with the jutting shape of the cliff. Naturally this theme is the energizing force of the great triangle that gives the group its monumental character. Far from being artificial byplay, Falconet's organization is an inherent element of his total concept. It has been seen that the sculptor had previously explored, in Saint-Roch, the dramatic possibilities of a large scale, theatrically conceived staging. More particularly, he had already experimented with the emotional effect of a subject cast in a wild, rocky setting, rendered even more fearsome by the presence of a large serpent. Falconet's fascination for unusually striking staging and his new sense of heroics, inspired by the heady legend of a demigod-like czar, led him to endow his monument with a dynamic power which produced the first epic equestrian statue of modern history.

The saying that the French do not have *l'âme épique* is especially applicable to the eighteenth century. Of course, this century was not wanting in soul-stirring drama. But most of the violent emotionalism which permeates La Chaussée's tragedies, Prévost's novels, Greuze's genre scenes, Vernet's shipwrecks, and for that matter, Falconet's own *Milo of Crotona*, was centered around the concept of pathos. At the time when the eighteenth century was searching for new sources of strong feeling, it was left to Falconet to channel some of its groping emotionalism into the expression of a completely different state of the soul: the epic drama. The revolutionary character of *Peter the Great* did not escape the perspicacious mind of Diderot. Referring to what he called Falconet's "epic poem," in a letter written to the sculptor on December 6, 1773, he comments: "I knew that you were a very skillful man, but may I be stricken dead if I suspected that you had anything like that in your head."

POSTSCRIPT

THE SURPRISING scope of Falconet's talent, which astounded Diderot in 1773, had already been suspected by Lemoyne some forty years earlier. After knowing Falconet for a year as his pupil, Lemoyne is reported to have told him that if he wanted to, he could be as simple as Bouchardon, as true as Pigalle, and as warm as Lemoyne himself. It is certain that one does not encounter very often artists capable of creating works as diametrically opposed as *Peter the Great* and *Pygmalion*. In fact, it is possible to continue, almost indefinitely, listing Falconet's "contrasts," opposing, for instance, the delicate elegance of his biscuits to the somber drama of his Calvary, or his Bernini-like Glory to his close-to-Canova *Winter*. One can, of course, demonstrate through some of Falconet's most prominent works that his development followed a "logical" sequence, leading from late Baroque-Rococo (i.e. *Milo*) to *lucidity Louis XV* (i.e. *The Bather*), and from *lucidity Louis XV* to a style bordering first on Neoclassicism (i.e. *Apelles and Campaspe*) and then on pre-Romanticism (i.e. *Peter the Great*). But however "logical," such a sequence must be understood as a broad generalization. It fails to take into account the overlappings, the revivals, and the anticipations that so frequently mark the evolution of Falconet's style. The unpredictable occurrence and the diversity of his many tendencies doubtless express a deep intellectual curiosity and, perhaps, a touch of restlessness. In these qualities, which are also present in his profuse writings, one can probably discern the first signs of the Romantic syndrome that will spread among the artists of the early nineteenth century. It is certain, for example, that Falconet was deeply aware of the stagnating effect of social conformity and that, on occasion, he expressed this awareness with a quasi-Baudelairian sense of "spleen." Thus, in the preface to his translation of Pliny, he writes:

> By dint of precaution, prudence, and excessive urbanity, we are in general colorless, without physiognomy, and without character. We all look alike, and the more we look like each other, the less we shall succeed to resemble anything: we are *bloodless* and *cowardly* could very well have said Montaigne . . . We have nothing but the physiognomy of fashion and never our own; and by contagion, we are always false, or at any rate weak. The contagion of custom is the best excuse for weak or spoiled temperaments.

But the sculptor does not wish to end this statement on a defeatist note. He adds:

> . . . let us abandon disguise to the weakness and the shame of those who understandably fear to appear as they really are. We are in the century of light, in the century in which, at any rate, a daring search for light becomes a crime only among those who fear light . . .

It can be seen that one should not unduly magnify the "Romantic" aspect of the sculptor's character: historically speaking, Falconet is neither a Romantic nor a revolutionary. To be sure, he is fully aware of the uncertainties of the artist's fate, but he does not claim for himself a special niche in society. When he describes (as related in the *Revue de Paris* of November 1842) his meeting in a tavern of Rouen with Frédéric Leroy, an eighteenth-century precursor of the nineteenth-century alcoholic bohemian painters, he is unmistakably moved by Leroy's pathetic behavior. Nevertheless, the tottering, daubing wretch is for Falconet first of all a curiosity: the philosophically intriguing case of shapeless bits of talent surviving in the midst of turpitude and misery. The sculptor feels really alien to this tragedy and fails to recognize in it any kind of symbol of the creative man's fate, in the Romantic sense of the concept. The authenticity of this colorful episode, which is reported by the litterateur Arsène Houssaye, is subject to caution. Nevertheless, it underlines an unquestionable fact: Falconet always remains the eighteenth-century artist-craftsman-philosopher, questioning everything, doubting everything, but also reconciling himself pragmatically to the unavoidable facts of life of his profession.

No eighteenth-century sculptor ever sensed more keenly than Falconet the variegated nature of his cultural milieu. Equaling or surpassing the talent of such men as Bouchardon, Pigalle, and Lemoyne, he emerges as the most engrossingly many-sided eighteenth-century sculptor before Houdon. In this light, it would have been gratifying to be able to underscore the far-reaching significance of Falconet's influence. But facts do not quite correspond to expectations. It is true that his *Cupid* and his *Bather* have never been forgotten. It is also true that his biscuits attained a European fame and provided a stylistic focus for his Sèvres collaborators, such as Duru and Le Riche, as well as for Boizot, his successor in the directorship of the factory sculpture studio. But the *Jean-Jacques of sculpture* loathed teaching. Perhaps for this reason the young artists who spent some time working under him, outside of Sèvres, who could presumably have pursued some of his other tendencies — for instance, Berruer, Lecomte, and Sénéchal — do not reflect his influence. This is even true of Mademoiselle Collot. Later, because of the razing of several of the Marquise de Pompadour's châteaux, the destruction of Falconet's ensemble at Saint-Roch, and the geographical remoteness of his *Peter the Great*, most of his non-Sèvres achievements were to be increasingly forgotten. All in all, Falconet did not leave any direct aesthetic heirs. His coherent strength, his subtlety, his elegance, his lyrical élan, and the integrity of his craftsmanship belong to the fabric of the French sculptural tradition, but his immortality as an artist remains confined to his own works.

APPENDIX

Falconet's *Reflections on Sculpture*

IN HIS PUBLISHED works, Falconet likes to remind his readers that he is not a writer, but a sculptor, and he often requests them to disregard his literary style. In a translation, one would be readily willing to comply with this wish if one could totally disregard the question of the sculptor's style — and that of his grammar — without coloring or losing his meaning. This would be an almost impossible task, for Falconet's style shows a self-contradictory pattern of qualities and shortcomings reminiscent of the contrasts that have been so graphically noted in Diderot's 1765 *Salon* portrayal of his personality (see Chap. I). Falconet is doubtless capable, on occasion, of coining a pithily lucid, eloquent phrase, and a sentence such as *"je n'approuve pas que l'artiste se livre à un beau rêve que les spectateurs ne pourraient pas faire avec lui"* (*Réflexions sur la sculpture*) brings to mind the poetic imperative of a manifesto. But, without attempting a literary analysis, one is forced to observe that his style is not always characterized by such inspired leanness; far from it — it often shows a tendency toward meandering rationalizations and endless qualifications, weighted down, and occasionally seriously obscured, by antiquarian footnotish pedantry and an autodidact's colloquialisms. Falconet is not easy to translate and not always easy to understand.

His writing, however, cannot be ignored. No eighteenth-century author ever gave a fuller and more passionate embodiment to the "artist's point of view," and few eighteenth-century authors — including Diderot — ever approached aesthetic problems with a comparably original insight. Admittedly, Falconet's important thoughts are often hidden in his many footnotes or in some apparently unrelated texts (his 1772 translation of Pliny's *Naturalis historia* provides a particularly good example). Falconet's "gems" are scattered amidst constellations of pseudo-scholarly digressions, historical anecdotes, argumentative points, angry rebuttals, and a great variety of criticisms. It must be pointed out that his criticisms frequently have a great intrinsic interest, as in such short essays as *Sur un article d'un certain journal, Sur une opinion de M. Lessing, Réponse à M. Mengs, Errata de quelques parcelles d'un excellent ouvrage*, which involve men like Linguet, Lessing, Mengs, and Voltaire. If one looks, however, for a "structured" exposition of Falconet's ideas, one must recognize that the *Réflexions sur la sculpture* (his first significant publication), although somewhat less entertaining, occupies a unique position in his writing. It is his most extensive, most coherent, and his least often self-interrupted discourse on his own art, composed without any discernible argumentative antagonism (if one excepts the competitive bias spurred by the art of the ancients which, one must note, is here less pronounced than in the sculptor's *Observations sur la statue de Marc-Aurèle*, 1771). It must be added that the *Réflexions sur la sculpture* is the most important statement on sculpture, visualized as a living and active art, of the time (Winckelmann's writings belong to a somewhat different category). Its eminent position continuously maintained by its publication in Diderot's very widely consulted *Encyclopedia* (where it was first published in 1761), the *Réflexions* was often quoted and paraphrased; and it was republished in Watelet's authoritative *Dictionnaire des Arts* (1792), as well as in each of the four editions of Falconet's complete works. The present translation is the first into English since that of 1777 by W. Foote, which appeared before Falconet had made several significant additions to his original text. With the exception of a few unimportant deletions, decided upon for the sake of clarity, Falconet's text is given here in its entirety. It is based on the 1787 edition of his *Oeuvres* (Paris: Didot et Jombert, v. 3, pp. 1-46), the last edition of the sculptor's writings published during his lifetime.

REFLECTIONS ON SCULPTURE

by Etienne-Maurice Falconet

(NOTE: If there is some truth in my view, it will be for the good of art. If I have sometimes been mistaken and if I have caught my errors in time, it will again be for the good of art. For the sake of young artists, I should like no one to be content to censor my errors without basing this censoring on solid proof.

As for the literary side of my essay, since the style of an artist carries absolutely no weight in the field of letters, my mistakes in this realm will not be contagious.)

. . . Sculpture, after history, is the most durable depository of the virtues and foibles of men. If the statue of Venus is the object of a stupid and dissolute cult, the statue of Marcus Aurelius is a monument famous by the homage paid to a benefactor of humanity.

The art of sculpture, by showing us the deification of vices, gives even more relief to the horrors which history has transmitted to us. On the other hand, the precious traits which remain to us of these rare men, who should have lived as long as their statues, revive in us the feeling of a noble emulation elevating our soul to the virtues which have prevented these great men from being forgotten by mankind . . .

The most worthy aim of sculpture, if one looks at it from a moral point of view, is therefore to perpetuate the memory of illustrious men and to give us models of virtue which are so much the more effective since the men who had these qualities can no longer be the objects of our envy. We have the portrait of Socrates and we venerate it. Who knows if we would have the courage to love Socrates if he were living among us?

Sculpture has yet another aim, apparently less useful. It is when it is concerned with subjects of simple decoration or pleasure, but then this does not make it less capable of elevating the soul to good or evil. . . . A sculptor, as well as a writer, is therefore worthy of praise or criticism according to the wholesomeness or licentiousness of his subjects.

By aiming at the imitation of the aspect of the human body, sculpture should not limit itself to depict a cold likeness or to represent man such as he would have appeared before the vivifying breath which gave him life. This type of truth, even if it were well reproduced, would excite by its exactness only a praise as cold as its likeness, and the soul of the onlooker would not be moved. It is the living, animated, passionate nature which the sculptor must express in marble, bronze, stone, etc.

Everything which is for the sculptor an object of imitation must be for him a continual object of study. This study, enlightened by genius, led by taste and reason, executed with precision, encouraged by the benevolent attention of rulers and by the advice and praise of great artists, will produce masterpieces similar to the precious monuments which have escaped unscathed from the barbary of the centuries. Thus, the sculptors who will not content themselves only with a tribute of praise which these sublime monuments, as a matter of fact, legitimately deserve, but who will study them in depth and will find in them standards for their own productions, will acquire the superiority which we so admire in Greek statues. If the works of our living sculptors could be mentioned as a proof of my thinking, they would be found in the gardens of Choisy (*Note:* a statue representing Cupid by Bouchardon) and in those of Sans-Souci (*Note:* a Mercury and a Venus by Mr. Pigalle).

The beautiful statues of antiquity will not be our only nourishment but also all the productions of genius, whatever they may be. The reading of Homer, that sublime painter, will elevate the soul of the artist and will imprint upon him so strongly an image of greatness and majesty that most of the objects which surround him will appear considerably diminished for him.

The greatest, the most sublime, the most singular creations of the sculptor's genius must express only the possible relationships of nature, of its effects, its accidents, its surprises; that is to say that beauty, what one may even call ideal beauty in sculpture as well as in painting, must be a summary of the real beauty of nature. There is an essential kind of beauty, but this beauty is scattered in different parts of the universe. To feel, to assemble, to bring together, to choose, to even conceive a few diverse aspects of this beauty, either in a type of figure like Apollo or in the ordering of a composition like the bold conceptions of Lanfranco, Correggio, Rubens, and other great masters of composition, is to express through art the beauty which one calls ideal beauty but whose principles are based on nature.

Above all, sculpture is the enemy of these forced attitudes that nature disavows and that several artists used unnecessarily, only to show that they knew how to handle at will all the problems of drawing. It is equally the enemy of the draperies whose only richness lies in a superfluous ornamentation due to a bizarre arrangement of folds. Finally, it is the enemy of over-studied compositional contrasts and too-artificial a distribution of light and shade. One could claim in vain that it is a great compositional scheme: in reality, it is nothing but disorder and a definite consequence of the sculptor's indecision and of the little effect of the subject on his soul. The more visible are the efforts which are made to move us, the less we are moved. Whereupon, it must be concluded that when the artist uses fewer means to produce an effect, he has more merit in producing it, and the onlooker is more likely to be moved by the impression which the artist wants to make on him. It is by the simplicity of such means that the great works of Greece have been created as though to serve eternally as models for the artists. . . .

Sculpture involves fewer tasks than painting, but those which it proposes to accomplish, which are common to both arts, are the most difficult to achieve, that is: expression, the science of contours, the difficult art of draping and of differentiating various types of fabric.

Sculpture has difficulties which are peculiar to it.

1 A sculptor cannot be excused from any part of his study by using shades, recessions, turns, and foreshortening.

2 If he has succeeded in composing and rendering well his work as seen from one point of view, he has satisfied only a part of his operation, since this work has as many points of view as there are points in the space which surrounds it (*Note:* This simple truth was carried very far by a few artists. It was even the cause of a rather ridiculous bit of sophistry in painting. Some sculptors claimed that a single statue showing several attitudes when one turns around it proves that sculpture surpasses painting. What power in these sculptors' reasoning! . . . On the other hand, Giorgione claimed that painting surpasses sculpture in this respect, since without moving one can see in a painting at one glance all the aspects and the different movements possible for a man . . . "He painted a nude man seen from the back; before him some very limpid water showed by reflection his front side; a polished armor showed the left side of the figure, while a mirror showed its right side. . ." (Vasari, *Vita di Giorgione*). We were not told if this cleverly inventive work was considered a convincing proof of Giorgione's contention. . . .

But I should not want to state however, like Mr. Laugier, that "perfection of drawing is the only merit of sculpture, and that no matter how much study the sculptor can give to the precision and to the elegance of his contours, he can hardly ever succeed in creating any illusion about the hardness and rigidity of the materials he must use." (See *Manière de bien juger des ouvrages de peinture*, p. 248.) If I had reasoned in this manner about sculpture and . . . if I were placed in front of the Laocoön and the Apollo, and if I were asked whether my soul is not impressed with any sense of illusion or whether these objects are works of sculpture or not, I would feel some shame at having authored such a judgment).

3 A sculptor must have an imagination as strong as that of a painter, I do not say as abundant. Moreover, his genius requires a tenacity capable of raising him above the discouragement which can be caused by the techniques, the weariness, the slowness of his operations. Genius cannot be acquired, it is developed, extended, and strengthened by practice. A sculptor uses his genius less often than a painter: another difficulty, since a work of sculpture must be endowed with genius as much as a work of painting.

4 Since the sculptor is deprived of the seductive charm of color, what intelligence must he not display in order to attract attention? In order to keep this attention, what precision, what truth, what choice of expression, must he not use in his works?

Since the work of a sculptor is most often composed of a single figure, in which it is not possible for him to combine the different factors which originate interest in a painting, one must require from a sculptor not only the interest which results from his work as a whole, but also the interest of each of its separate parts. Painting, independently from the variety of color, attracts the onlooker by different groupings, attributes, ornaments, expressions of several figures participating in the subject. Painting interests us by its backgrounds, by the setting of the scene, by its general effect: in one word, it impresses through its totality. But most often, the sculptor has only one word to say; this word must have energy.

Some very skillful sculptors have certainly borrowed the help of color which is so much to the advantage of painting. Examples of this are provided by Rome and Paris. Undoubtedly, materials of various colors, used with skill, could produce some picturesque effects. But when they are distributed without harmony, the combination renders the sculpture disagreeable and even shocking. The brilliance of gilding, the unexpected confrontation of the discordant colors of different types of marble will dazzle the populace always attracted by glitter, but a man of taste will be repelled. The best thing would be to use gold, bronze, and different types of marble only for decorative purposes and not to take away from sculpture *per se* its true character. Thus, sculpture, by remaining within the boundaries which are prescribed to it, will not lose any of its advantages, something which would certainly occur if it wanted to use all the elements proper to painting. . . .

But if the means of color, which properly belongs to painting, is an advantage for it, how many difficulties does this art not have which are completely alien to sculpture.

The ability to create an illusion through color is in itself a very great difficulty. The rarity of this talent only proves it too well. The more objects the painter has to represent than the sculptor, the more need for special studies. The true imitation of sky, of water, of landscape, of different moments of the day, of various effects of light, and the rule of lighting a painting only from one single source of light demand a knowledge and a kind of work which are essential for painters and from which a sculptor is entirely exempt (*Note: Matter and rays of light react continually upon each other: matter on rays of light by emitting them, reflecting them, and refracting them; and rays of light on matter by heating it and by giving to its parts a vibrating movement, etc.*

These are the observations of the great Newton on the effects of light; and it is precisely what the great painters who lived before him had observed and practiced. The artists did not owe this important principle of art to any philosopher; and most of them who applied it in a superior fashion could not have been able to read Newton. But, like him, they were reading nature: the former wrote about it, the latter painted it. Thus, when you will be told that it is the philosopher who holds the scepter which must rule the arts and that this scepter must never fall from his hands, you must make an exception for the art of painting.)

Painting can still be pleasing even if it is deprived of the enthusiasm and the genius which characterize it. But the productions of sculpture, when they are not supported by these two foundations, are insipid. Let genius inspire these two arts equally, nothing will prevent them from being in the most intimate union, in spite of the differences which exist in some of their procedures. Even if these arts are not similar in everything, there always remains a family likeness. . . .

If, through an error, of which one fortunately sees few examples, a sculptor were to take for enthusiasm and genius the unreasonable impetuosity which possessed Borromini and Meissonier, let him be persuaded that such excesses, far from embellishing objects, move them away from the truth and serve only to represent the disorders of the imagination. Although these two artists were not sculptors, they can be mentioned as dangerous examples, because the same spirit which leads the architect also leads the painter and the sculptor. The artist whose approach is simple is in the open. He exposes himself to be judged so much the more easily that he uses no *vain* prestige to escape criticism and often to mask his lack of achievement in such a manner. Thus, let us not call *beauty*, in any work, that which would only dazzle the eye and tend to corrupt taste. This taste, praised so rightly in the productions of the human spirit, generally appears to be, in my opinion, the result of the work of common sense on our ideas. When they are too lively, common sense knows how to dampen them and restrain them. When they are too languid, it knows how to bring them to life. It is to this happy temperament that sculpture, as well as all the arts which have been invented to please us, owes its true beauty, the only beauty which will endure.

Since sculpture requires the most rigorous precision, a laxness in drawing would be less bearable there than in painting. This does not imply that Raphael and Domenichino have not been very accurate and knowledgeable draughtsmen and that all great painters do not look at drawing as essential in art. But, at least, a painting that would not be dominated by drawing could still stimulate interest by other qualities. The proof of this lies in some of the women painted by

Rubens, who, in spite of their Flemish character and their lack of correctness, will always appear pleasing by the charm of their color. Represent them in sculpture, with the same kind of drawing, their charm will be considerably diminished, if not entirely destroyed. The experiment would be much worse if one were to use a few figures of Rembrandt.

Why is it less permissible for a sculptor than for a painter to neglect some of the aspects of his art? It is perhaps because of three considerations: the length of time that the artist devotes to his work — we cannot bear for a man to have spent long years to execute a common work; the price of the material used — what a difference between a piece of canvas and a block of marble!; the survival of the work — everything around the marble vanishes but the marble remains, even when broken, its fragments still carry to the future centuries something to praise or to criticize.

After indicating the aim and the general system of sculpture, one must still consider it as subjected to particular laws which the artist must know in order not to violate them or to stretch them beyond their limits.

It would be stretching these laws too far if one were to say that sculpture cannot rise to great heights in its composition because of the sculptor's necessity to be ruled by the size of his block of marble. One need only look at the *Gladiator* and the *Atalante*. These Greek figures well prove that the block of marble obeys when the sculptor knows how to command.

But this freedom which, so to speak, empowers the sculptor to make the marble grow must not go so far as to encumber the external appearance of his figures by tiresome details which are contrary to the action and movement represented. The work, by standing out from a background of air, tree, or architecture, must assert itself unequivocally from the farthest distinguishable point possible. The lights and shades widely distributed will also concur to determine the main forms and the general effect. No matter the distance from which the Apollo and the Gladiator are seen, their action is not doubtful. . . .

Among the difficulties of sculpture, there is one which is well known and which requires the greatest care from the artist. It is the impossibility to have second thoughts once his marble is blocked out and to introduce any essential changes in the composition or in any one of its parts. This is a strong reason which compels him to decide on his model and to conceive it so that he can undertake the work on his marble with assurance. This is why, in the case of large works, most sculptors make their models, or at least sketch them out on the very spot where the projected statue is to be placed. In this way, they determine with certainty the lights, the shades, and the desired total view of their work, which could create an excellent effect when composed by the light of their atelier and a very bad one when placed in its final location.

But this difficulty goes even further. I am supposing that, once his model is decided upon, the sculptor has a moment of sleepiness or delirium. If he works then, I can see him very well mutilating some important part of his figure in the belief that he is following and even perfecting his model. The next day, his head cleared, he recognizes the disorder of the preceding day without being able to remedy it.

Happy advantages of painting! It is not subjected to this rigorous law. The painter can change, correct, rework his canvas at will; at worst, he can paint over it or even take another one. Can the sculptor handle his marble in the same manner? If he had to begin his work anew, could his loss of time, his fatigue, and his expenses be compared to those of the painter?

Moreover, if the painter has traced correct lines, established the proper shades and lights, a different point of view or a different lighting will not rob him of the fruit of his skill and of his care. But in a work of sculpture, composed so as to produce harmonious lights and shades, let the daylight which came from the left come from the right or from the bottom instead of from the top, and you will no longer find any effects, or they will be only unpleasant ones if the artist did not know how to provide for different types of lighting. Moreover, very often, the sculptor by wanting to create a work that can be seen from all points of view is risking true beauty for the sake of a mediocre harmony. . . .

When a sculptor has overcome these difficulties, the artists and the true connoisseurs are undoubtedly grateful to him, but how many people, even among those who love our arts, not knowing the difficulties of the sculptor, will not recognize his merit at having overcome them.

The nude figure is the principal object of the sculptor's study. The foundations of his study are the knowledge of bone structure, of external anatomy, and the assiduous imitation of all the parts and of all the movements of the human body. The school of Paris and that of Rome require this exercise and help the students to acquire this necessary knowledge. But since nature can have its imperfections, and since the young student by dint of seeing and copying these imperfections must naturally transpose them into his own works, it is necessary for him to have a dependable guide to make him learn the correct proportions and beautiful forms.

Greek statues are the most dependable guides. They are and always will be the rule of precision, gracefulness, and nobility, since they are the most perfect representation of the human body. If one is to be content with a superficial examination, these statues will not seem extraordinary nor even difficult to imitate; but the understanding and attentive artist will discover in some of them the most profound knowledge of drawing and all the energy of nature. Thus, it is the sculptors who have studied the antique figures the most and with the greatest selectivity who have distinguished themselves the most. I say *with selectivity*, and I consider this remark well founded.

However beautiful the antique statues are, they are human productions and consequently susceptible of having the weaknesses of humanity. Therefore it would be dangerous for the artist to admire indiscriminately everything which is called antique. Thus, after admiring in certain works of antiquity some so-called marvels which are not there, he would attempt to appropriate them for himself and would not in turn be admired. He must learn the beauties and the faults of the ancients through an enlightened, judicious, and unprejudiced selectivity, and, after appreciating them, he must walk in their footsteps with even more confidence, since then they will always lead him to greatness. It is in this judicious type of selectivity that appears the clarity of the mind, and the talent of the sculptor is always proportionate to this clarity. Even a mediocre knowledge of our arts is sufficient to see that the Greek artists also had their moments of slumber and coldness. The same taste prevailed, but knowledge was not the same among all artists. The pupil of an excellent sculptor could have his master's manner without having his head.

Among the figures of antiquity, the most proper to offer great principles for the study of the nude are the *Gladiator*, the *Apollo*, the *Laocoön*, the *Farnese Hercules*, the *Torso*, the *Antinous*, the *group of Castor and Pollux*, the *Hermaphrodite*, and the *Venus of Medici*. I think that I can find the trace of these great works in the productions of some of our greatest modern sculptors. In Michelangelo, one can see a profound study of the *Laocoön*, of the *Hercules*, and of the *Torso*. Can one doubt while looking at the works of François Duquesnoy that he has not greatly studied the *Gladiator*, the *Apollo*, the *Antinous*, *Castor and Pollux*, *Venus*, and the *Hermaphrodite*? Puget undoubtedly has studied the *Laocoön* and other antique statues, but his principal master was nature whose structure and movements he could see continuously in the convicts of Marseille. Thus the habit of seeing objects which are more or less related to the true system of the arts can form taste or stop its progress. In our case, we only see clothing designed without regard to the beauty of the human body; what an effort is required from us in order to remove the mask, to see and know nature, and to express in our works only the beauty that is independent from fashion whatever it may be! It is up to the great artists, to whom all of nature is open, to formulate the laws of good taste . . . : they must not receive any law from the caprices and bizarreness of fashion.

I must not forget here an important observation on the subject of the ancients. It is essential in relation to the manner in which their sculptors represented flesh. They were so little concerned with details that often they neglected the wrinkles and the movements of the skin in the places where it stretches and folds over according to the action of the limbs. This aspect of sculpture has perhaps been carried to a higher degree of perfection today. An example, taken from the works of Puget, will show if my observation is justified.

In what Greek statue does one find a feeling for the folds of the skin, for the softness of the flesh, and for the fluidity of the blood, rendered as excellently as in the productions of this famous modern sculptor? Who does not see blood circulating in the veins of the *Milo* of Versailles? And what sensitive man would not be prone to be fooled when seeing the flesh of the *Andromeda* . . ., while one can mention many beautiful figures from the antique lacking a comparable reality? Therefore, it would be somehow ungrateful on our part if, acknowledging the sublimity of Greek sculpture in so many other respects, we would refuse to admire an accomplishment which is far superior in the works of a French artist. . . .

We have seen that it is the imitation of natural objects submitted to the principles of the ancients that constitutes the true beauty of sculpture. But the most profound study of the figures of antiquity, the most perfect knowledge of muscles, the precision of the line, the very art of rendering the harmonious areas of the skin and of expressing the structure of the human body, this knowledge, I say, is only made for the eyes of the artists and for those of a very small number of connoisseurs. But since sculpture does not exist only for those who practice it or for those who are knowledgeable about it, the sculptor must, in order to deserve unanimous praise, add to the studies which are necessary for him an even greater talent. This talent, so essential and so rare, although it seems to be available to all artists, is *feeling*. It must be present in all their productions. It is feeling which gives them life: if the other studies are the basis for these productions, feeling alone is their soul. Acquired knowledge is an individual matter, but feeling belongs to all men. It is universal: in this respect all men are the judges of our works.

To render the forms of the body without including feeling is only to fulfill one's goal half way. To want to scatter feeling everywhere, without regard for precision, is only to make sketches and only to produce dreams whose impression will be dissipated when one no longer sees the work, or even when one looks at it for too long a time. To combine these two elements (but what a difficult task!) is to reach the sublime in sculpture.

RELIEFS

Since relief is a very interesting part of sculpture and since the ancients did not perhaps leave enough examples showing all the means of producing them, I am going to try to present a few ideas on this type of work.

Essentially, one must distinguish between two types of reliefs, that is, low relief and high relief, and one must determine their usage and prove that both of them must be equally admissible according to circumstances.

On an unadorned architectural plane, a panel, a column, a vase, objects which are not supposed to be broken and which do not allow any recesses, a high relief with many planes and with the figures of the first plane completely detached from the background would create the worst possible effect, because it would destroy the harmony of the architecture. The distant planes of this relief would suppose and would suggest a recess where there should not be any; they would break through the building, at least it would appear so to the eye. Therefore, in such cases, one needs a very low relief, with very few planes: a work difficult to execute because of the required mastery and softness of the nuances which create its harmony. The only effect of this relief is that which results from the architecture to which it must be entirely subordinated. One must understand without having to say it that the *subject* and the *style* must also participate in the union with the architecture.

But there are places where a high relief can be used very effectively and where the planes and the protrusions, far from creating disorder, will only add to the semblance of truth which every imitation of nature must have. These places can usually be found on an altar or on such other architectural element which can be visualized as having openings or be susceptible of recession, with sufficient dimensions, since a low relief in a large area would not create any kind of effect when viewed from a distance. Such places and dimensions are the opening of a stage where the sculptor can create any recesses he might want in order to give to the scene he is representing all the action, the play, and interest which the subject requires from his art, yet always obeying the laws of reason, good taste, and precision. This is also a type of work through which one can understand more easily the relationship between sculpture and painting and through which one can show that the principles that both arts derive from nature are absolutely the same. . . . Those who think that this type of relief will produce a blinking effect are not aware of the means available to a knowing sculptor in order to avoid this problem. . . .

Because other men who lived several centuries before us have tried only a few steps in this direction, should we not dare to go beyond! . . . One can display a great deal of erudition in proving that the reliefs from antiquity are a precious source from which we can learn about the *costume of the ancients*. Who has ever doubted this? But this question has no bearing on pictorial conception or rather *sculptural* conception about which I am only speaking here.

. . . We who have supposedly carried our painting beyond that of the ancients as far as the understanding of chiaroscuro, the magic of color, the rendering of large subjects, and the intricacies of composition, shall we not dare to take the same flight into the realm of sculpture? Bernini, Legros, Algardi, Melchiorre Caffà, Angelo Rossi, have shown us that it is up to good taste and genius to extend the narrow circle to which the ancients have limited themselves in creating their reliefs. These great modern artists have successfully freed themselves from an authority which is admissible only in so far as it is reasonable. . . .

I do not want to leave any doubts as to the judgment which I am making on antique reliefs. I find there, as well as in the beautiful statues, a great manner of execution in each particular detail and the most noble simplicity of composition. But however noble this composition may be, it does not contribute in any way to the illusion of a painting, and the relief must always seek to create this illusion, since this illusion is nothing but an imitation of natural objects.

If the relief is very high, one should not fear a possible lack of harmony between the figures of the first plane and those of the background. The sculptor will know how to create a harmony between the smallest and highest protrusions: he needs only a location, good taste, and genius. But it must be acknowledged that this harmony must be required and that we must not oppose it because we do not find it in the reliefs of antiquity.

A softness created by monotonous lights and shadows recurring in most of these works cannot be called harmony. The eye sees cut-out figures pasted on a board, and the eye is revolted. . . .

Some skillful artists, however, might think that a relief must not pretend to be anything but a drawing highlighted with a little shade to show some protrusions, and the idea of pretending to be a painting might appear to them excessive. The reason which can perhaps be given for this point of view might be the lack of success of this type of relief when attempted by some of our sculptors. But has it been carefully considered whether this lack of success comes from the art or from the artist? Is the beautiful relief of Attila by Algardi in the same category? Do the reliefs of the students who enter prize competitions not have the approval of the Academy when these reliefs combine with other qualities a happy understanding of wisely varied planes, that is, as much as sculpture can allow it without reaching a so-called freedom that would be much more shocking than able to convey illusion? For I do not approve the artist yielding to a beautiful dream that the onlookers could not possibly share. . . .

One would be badly defending the cause of the antique reliefs if one were to say that this background which so unpleasantly stops the eye is made up of a serene body of air freed from anything which might obstruct the figures, since when one paints or draws from a relief one takes great care to trace the shadow which edges the figures and which indicates so well that they are pasted on to this board which one calls background, thereby proving that one does not really think that this background is a body of air. It is true that this ridiculous imitation is practiced so as to reveal that the drawing was executed after the sculpture. Thus, the sculptor is the only one to blame for having given to his work a ridiculous element which must be reproduced in the copies or imitations made from it.

Whatever the location and whatever the projection of the relief, it must be in harmony with the architecture, and its subject, composition, and draperies must be consistent with the character of this architecture. Thus, the virile austerity of the Tuscan order will allow only simple subjects and compositions, the costumes will have to be ample and with few folds. But the Corinthian and Composite orders require a breadth of composition and looseness and lightness of fabric . . .

Since the rules of composition and of expressiveness are the same for reliefs as for paintings, the principal actors must occupy the most interesting spot of the scene and must be placed so as to receive a sufficient amount of light which will attract, arrest, and settle the eye on them as in a painting. . . . This central light will not be interrupted by any detail of hard and narrow shadows which would only produce spottiness and would destroy the harmony. Little threads of light that might appear in great masses of shadow would equally destroy this harmony.

There should be no foreshortening in the forward planes, especially if the extremities of these foreshortenings were to jut forward; they would only create an unbearable thinness. Losing their natural length, these parts would become unbelievable and would look like pegs sunken into the figures.

Thus, in order not to shock the eye, the freely protruding limbs must, as much as possible, be directed toward the background. Placed in such a manner, they will create another advantage: they will be sustained by their own mass. Let us observe however, that even when they are free, they should not be too closely attached to the background, for this would distort the proportions of the figures and the relation of the planes.

Let the figures of the second plane as well as any of their parts not be as protruding or as firmly executed as those of the first plane. This is also true for the figures of the other planes according to their position in depth. Even if one were to find any examples of such a uniformity of execution, even if it might occur in antique reliefs, one would have to consider such examples as showing a lack of understanding of the gradation which distance, air, and our eye naturally place between us and the objects surrounding us. In nature, as things recede from us, their forms become more blurred in relation to us: an observation so much the more essential that, in a relief, the relative distance between figures is far from real; those which one thinks are six or twelve feet further removed than the other are sometimes not any further apart than an inch. Therefore, it is only through a vagueness and blurring of execution, together with proportions diminishing according to the rules of perspective, that the sculptor will come closer to the truth and to the effect displayed by nature. It is also the only way to produce this harmony which sculpture cannot find and must not seek to find outside of the single color of its own substance.

Above all, it is necessary to avoid that each figure be encircled by a little edge of uniform width of shade which, by taking away the illusion of the protrusions and of the respective position in depth of these figures, would give them here also the appearance of figures flattened against each other and pasted on a board. One can avoid this defect by giving a sort of roundness to the edge of the figures and enough protrusion to their middle parts. Let the shadow carried from one figure to another appear to be carried naturally, that is, let these figures be on planes that are near enough so that the shadow of one may fall on the other, as though they were natural. It must be observed however that the planes of the principal figures, especially the ones which must express action, should not be confused but rather should be distinct enough and sufficiently apart in order to allow the figures to move easily.

When a figure in a foreground plane must appear to be isolated and detached from the other figures without really being so, one can oppose a shadow behind the lighted side of that figure and if possible a light area behind its shadow: a happy means which nature offers to the sculptor as well as to the painter in order to give movement and distance to their representation.

If the relief is made of marble, the resemblance to a painting will increase with the amount of variety the sculptor will introduce in the treatment of the different areas of his representation. Dull, rough-grained, or polished marble, used with understanding, can claim some similarity to color. The reflections cast from the polish of one drapery on another give lightness to the fabric and spread harmony in the composition.

If one were to doubt that the laws of reliefs are the same as those of painting, let one choose a painting by Poussin or Le Sueur and let a skillful sculptor make a model of it; it will be seen whether the result will not be a beautiful relief. These masters have brought sculpture and painting closer to each other because they have always represented their settings with truth and reason. Their figures are generally not far from each other and on very precise planes: a rigorous law which must be observed with scrupulous care in a relief. Finally, I repeat it, this type of sculpture is the least equivocal proof of the analogy existing between sculpture and painting. To break this relationship would be to degrade sculpture and to confine it only to statues . . . while nature offers to it, as well as to painting, the possibility of creating tableaux. Those readers who are not familiar with this appellation can consult Vasari and other Italian writers; they will see that a relief is called *quadro*, a term which as well as *tavola* signifies *tableau*. The Italians have been saying for over three hundred years *un quadro di bassorilievo* (a relief tableau). Let us not deserve the reproach of shrinking, impoverishing an art which our masters have handed down to us with the idea of its scope, and let us say, without entering into further details, that except for color, a high relief is *in sculpture* a difficult tableau. But whatever its difficulty and even its success, I do not claim to say that it creates the same illusion as a painting: I am only intimately convinced that it must borrow from painting or rather from nature all the means which are useful to it and which can help it to add the greatest possible interest to its composition. . . .

DRAPERIES

There remains for me to examine an aspect of sculpture about which artists do not perhaps agree completely, an aspect which is as interesting as it is difficult: it is the art of draping.

Let me imagine that a sculptor smitten by the simplicity of the beautiful antique draperies and revolted by some of the ingenious bizarreness of Bernini will adopt only the style of antique folds, and that another sculptor, seeing all types of draperies exemplified in nature, will feel free, as nature's imitator, to represent them all. It appears that these two points of view, which seem to be mutually exclusive, can be equally useful to sculpture, and that it would be detrimental if one would prevail over the other. Would it not be the same for the representative arts as for languages, which would be impoverished if one suppressed words that are the only signs standing for certain ideas? If one removed from sculpture certain means of imitation, would one not also impoverish it? Therefore, one should outlaw only the cold, heavy, extravagant, or out of place.

Draperies which are called wet draperies can well be introduced in sculpture where, when used without affectation, without skimpiness, according to the subject and the appropriateness, they allow to show the movements of the nude figure by making the forms more clearly felt, less awkward, and therefore more interesting.

Greek sculptors, fascinated by the beauty of the nude body, draped their figures with such fine fabric that it seemed to be wet and sometimes glued to the skin. Their way of life, their climate, their manner of dress, the fabric they used for their clothes, accustomed their eye and formed their taste. The garb of the women of the island of Cos was made of such transparent gauze that the nude forms could be seen through it, and the Greek sculptors were guided by this garb to represent their draperies. But since sculpture has the whole of nature as an object of imitation, and since nature has more than one kind of beauty, why should a sculptor slavishly follow one manner of draping that was used to fit a certain time, climate, and circumstances?

The great modern sculptors, such as François Duquesnoy, Puget, Algardi, Rusconi, Legros, Angelo Rossi, Sarrazin, and sometimes Bernini show us what beauty can be produced in sculpture by large draperies thrown in a grand manner. The sculptors from antiquity also show this, but seldom, so that one could criticize an exclusive taste for wet antique draperies by referring to the use of large draperies during the same period, such as those of Zeno at the Capitoline Palace, those of the little Flora in the same palace, whose folds are composed with the warmth of brilliant fabric, of Sardanapalus at the Clementine museum, and of Marius in the Negroni villa.

In the observations that one could make about the draperies of the ancients, one should not confuse the treatment of the surface with the arrangement and choice of the folds. If the treatment is sometimes tasteless, without skill or truth, the arrangement and the choice of the draperies are almost always knowledgeable and able to offer the most sublime lessons. One can see in the beautiful copy after the antique made by Legros in the Tuileries, the effect antique draperies can produce when they are treated so as to follow the truth of nature. All the artists who have seen the original of this figure know how much its execution is inferior to that of its copy; we can see what happens to the antique type of folds when they are in the hands of a great sculptor. The beautiful execution of the figures of the Fountain of the Innocents also shows what good use can be made of them. These figures are nymphs, and this type of drapery is fitting for them.

Let us dare to admit that the ancients have often neglected the study of this aspect of sculpture; but in our eyes they lose very little in comparison with what they have left for us to admire. No sculptor has the right to remain unaware of the fact that the chisel can succeed in the variety of work required by the different fabrics. Whatever they are, let us observe that the spacing and the number of folds should not be uniform, and that their projection and depth, which produce the shadows, should be harmoniously varied. Otherwise, the eye will be tired of the monotony such as one can see in the drapery of the Niobe Family, where the folds, unskillfully distributed and unrealistically executed, pretty much resemble cords, wood shavings, or pieces of bark arranged in an insipid way. Harmony is as necessary in sculpture as in music: the eyes are no more indulgent than the ears. . . .

Therefore, let the planes of each fold be disposed so as not to produce any sharp angle of light or shadow which, by standing out harshly, would shock the eye, destroy the restful continuity of the flesh areas, and Gothic figures, would present nothing but disunity in the details. . . .

But floating draperies should be outlawed. They interrupt the action, divide the interest, tire the eye, and prevent the principal object from being seen. An exception should be made however, for subjects and actions where the draperies have to be unavoidably agitated, such as the fall of Icarus, Apollo pursuing Daphne, etc. Then, these draperies, treated with great art and lightness, add to the interest and truthfulness of the action.

In a relief, they can also be successfully introduced to extend the pattern of lights and darks, link groups, and be useful in the staging of a composition. But if they are intersected in an opposite direction by a multitude of breaks, such as can be seen in some of the works of Bernini, then they look like rocks and completely destroy peace and harmony.

If these principles are founded on taste and on nature, the result is that a sculptor, by following them, could afford to stay away from any kind of particular system. But what does it matter to him? He must know that in art the search for truth does not recognize any particular authority. Let him have the courage to work for all times and all countries.

I have said that the arrangement of antique folds can give the most sublime lessons. It is therefore necessary, in order to form one's taste for draping figures after the best principles, to consult the antique draperies in the original rather than modern draperies, which are more varied and treated in a broader and less cold manner. This study must even be considered as essential for draping as the study of the muscles is for the nude.

Once these principles are recognized, they are applicable to all styles, and nature, which never loses its rights, will always offer variety and profitable lessons to the sculptor who will have learned from the antique how to shield himself against the abuses of different manners.

I have also said that the customs, the climate, the costume of the Greeks were the cause of their taste for clinging draperies. Therefore, one should not be surprised if broad draperies did not always succeed in pleasing them. It is for the same reason that one sees few of them in their painting: the Aldobrandini wedding, an antique painting, is composed and draped precisely as the statues and the reliefs of the same period.

We have the subject of Coriolanus, engraved after an antique painting found in the Thermae of Titus, in which the figures are very symmetrically arranged, the order and the styles of the folds are similar to those of antique statues. The paintings and the sculptures found in Herculaneum are in the same style.

If one still had doubts as to the success of broad draperies, one could, for the sake of reassurance, look at the figures of Legros, Rusconi, Angelo Rossi, which are in St. John in Lateran in Rome; the St. Andrew of François Duquesnoy in St. Peter; the St. Teresa of Bernini, whose Carmelite costume would have seemed alien to the effect and the looseness of a drapery which announces the various movements of the human body; in a word, so many other figures whose broad draperies are unanimously admired. If these sculptors had slavishly imitated the ancients and if they had not dared to try something for themselves, of how much beauty would we have been deprived? They could say with Tacitus: *what is today very ancient was formerly new, and what we are doing without following an example will serve as an example.* . . .

Translated by EDA MEZER LEVITINE

1. *J.-B. Lemoyne,* Falconet at the Age of Twenty-six. *Drawing, 1741.*
Private collection, Paris (L'OEil, Paris)

left: 2. J.-B. Lemoyne; Louis XV. Small bronze replica
of the destroyed statue of Bordeaux, 1766.
Musée des Arts Décoratifs, Bordeaux (Giraudon)

below: 3. M.-A. Collot, Falconet. Marble, 1768.
Hermitage, Leningrad (Archives Photographiques)

above: 4. Agesander, Athanodorus, Polydorus,
The Laocoön. Marble, ca. first century B.C.
The Vatican, Rome (Anderson-Giraudon)

left: 5. P. Puget, Milo of Crotona. Marble,
1682. Louvre, Paris (Archives Photographiques)

6. *Falconet, Milo of Crotona. Marble, 1754.*
About 70 cm. Louvre, Paris (Archives Photographiques)

right: 7. *Milo of Crotona,*
detail (Archives Photographiques)

below: 8. *Milo of Crotona,*
detail (Archives Photographiques)

opposite page: **9.** *Falconet, Allegory of Sculpture. Marble, ca. 1754. About 65 cm. Victoria and Albert Museum, London (Museum photo)*

right: **10.** *Michelangelo, The Delphic Sibyl. Fresco, 1508–12. Sistine Chapel, Rome (Anderson-Giraudon)*

below: **11.** *Allegory of Sculpture, detail (Museum photo)*

opposite page: 12. *Falconet,*
E. Dumont, A. Pajou, France
Embracing the Bust of Louis XV.
Marble, 1747–1779. About
150 cm. Palais Municipal,
Libourne (Bonny)

right: 13. *France Embracing the*
Bust of Louis XV, back view (Bonny)

14. *Falconet, Music. Marble, ca. 1752. About 200 cm.*
Louvre, Paris (Archives Photographiques)

15. *Music, detail (Archives Photographiques)*

left: **16.** *Falconet, The Menacing Cupid. Marble, 1757. About 90 cm. Louvre, Paris (Archives Photographiques)*

17. *Harpocrates. Engraving from O. van Veen, Theatro Moral de la Vida Humana, Antwerp, Verdussen, 1733, p. 59*

18. *J.-B. Lemoyne. Vertumnus and Pomona. Marble, 1760. Louvre, Paris (Giraudon)*

19. *Falconet, The Menacing Cupid, side view of statue shown in Fig. 16 (Archives Photographiques)*

DONNÉ AU MUSÉE DU LOUVRE
PAR L'ARCHITECTE AUGUSTE JOSEPH ROUDEVN
NÉ A PARIS LE 4 JUIN 1851
MORT A NAPLES, LE 25 FEVRIER 1855

20, 21, 22. *Falconet, The Bather. Marble, 1757.*
About 82 cm. Louvre, Paris (Archives Photographiques)

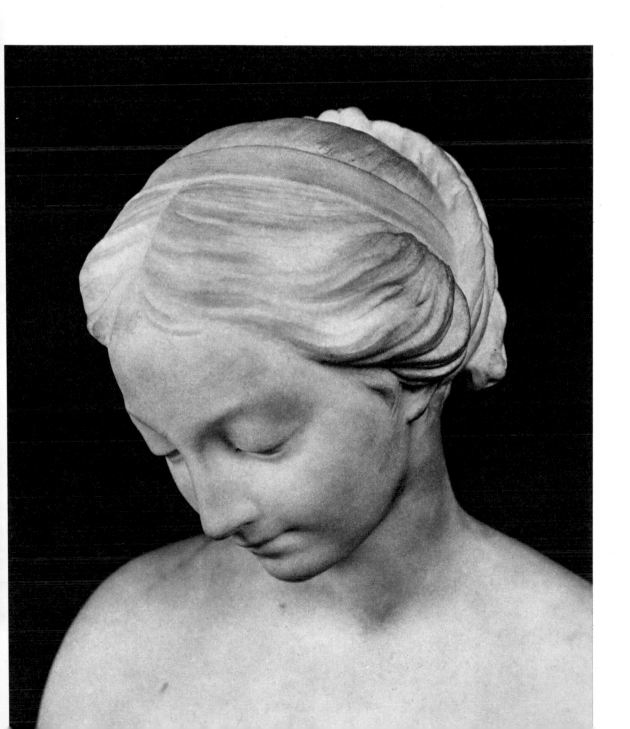

above: **23.** *Falconet (?),*
The Bather with the Rose. Marble,
ca. 1757. About 80 cm. Victoria and
Albert Museum, London (Museum photo)

lower right: **25.** *F. Lemoyne,*
The Bather. Painting, ca. 1724. Musée des
Beaux-Arts, Tours (Giraudon)

opposite page: **24.** *L.-S. Boizot, Bathing Nymph. Biscuit, 1774.*
Victoria and Albert Museum, London (Museum photo)

26. *Falconet, Sweet Melancholy.*
Terra-cotta, ca. 1761-1772. About
35 cm. Musée National de Céramique,
Sèvres (Cliché des Musées Nationaux)

27. *Falconet, Sweet Melancholy. Marble,*
1763. About 100 cm. Hermitage, Leningrad

30. *Falconet, Pygmalion and Galatea.*
Marble, ca. 1763. About 85 cm. Louvre,
Paris (Cliché des Musées Nationaux)

29. *F. Lemoyne, Pygmalion and Galatea.*
Painting, ca. 1729.
Musée des Beaux-Arts, Tours (Bulloz)

left: **31.** *Galatea, detail of statue shown in Fig. 30.* right: **32.** *Pygmalion, detail of statue shown in Fig. 30 (Cliché des Musées Nationaux)*

opposite page bottom: **33.** *G. de Saint-Aubin. View of the Salon of 1765. Drawing (detail) showing Falconet's entries. (From left to right: Sweet Melancholy; Friendship with the Heart; Winter; Apelles and Campaspe; Saint Ambrose, for the Church of the Invalides, now lost.) Cabinet des Dessins, Louvre, Paris (Giraudon)*

34. *Pygmalion and Galatea, back view of statue shown in Fig. 30 (Cliché des Musées Nationaux)*

35. *Falconet, Apelles and Campaspe. Marble, 1765.*
About 85 cm x 70 cm. Private collection (Arlaud)

upper left: **36.** Falconet, *Friendship with the Heart.*
Biscuit, 1764. About 35 cm. Manufacture Nationale
de Sèvres (Cliché des Musées Nationaux)

upper right: **37** Falconet, *Friendship.*
Plaster model, 1755. About 38 cm. Manufacture Nationale
de Sèvres (Cliché des Musées Nationaux)

left: **38.** Urania. Engraving from C. Ripa, Iconologie,
Amsterdam, Braakman, 1698, II, p. 364

39, 40. *Falconet, Winter.*
Marble, ca. 1763–1771. 140 cm. Hermitage, Leningrad

41, 42. *Winter, detail of head,*
detail of flowers. Hermitage, Leningrad

43. *Falconet, The Teaching of Love. Plaster model, 1763. About 31 cm. Manufacture Nationale de Sèvres (Cliché des Musées Nationaux)*

44. *The Teaching of Love, view from above of model shown in Fig. 43 (Cliché des Musées Nationaux)*

45. *Falconet, The Magic Lantern.*
Biscuit, 1757. About 15 cm.
Musée des Arts Décoratifs,
Paris (Museum photo)

46. *Falconet, The Wafers Lottery.*
Plaster model, 1757. About 15 cm.
Manufacture Nationale de Sèvres
(Cliché des Musées Nationaux)

47. *C.-N. Cochin, Country Fair. Engraving after F. Boucher, ca. 1736.*

48. *Falconet, Jupiter and Leda. Biscuit, 1764. About 32 cm.*
Victoria and Albert Museum, London (Museum photo)

49. *Falconet, The Opera Dance.*
Plaster model, 1765. About 12 cm.
Manufacture Nationale de Sèvres
(Cliché des Musées Nationaux)

50. *Falconet, The Schoolmistress.*
Biscuit, 1762. About 23 cm. Musée
des Arts Décoratifs, Paris (Museum
photo)

51. *Falconet, Silenus and the Bacchantes. Terra-cotta, 1759. About 18 cm. Musée National de Céramique, Sèvres (Cliché des Musées Nationaux)*

52. *View from above of a plaster model of the group illustrated in Fig. 51. Manufacture Nationale de Sèvres (Cliché Musées Nationaux)*

53. *Falconet, Erigone. Terra-cotta,*
ca. 1747–1759. About 27 cm.
Musée National de Céramique, Sèvres
(Cliché des Musées Nationaux)

54. *Falconet, The Fairy Urgèle.*
Terra-cotta, ca. 1766. About 20 cm.
Musée National de Céramique, Sèvres
(Cliché des Musées Nationaux)

55. *Falconet, The Menacing Cupid. Biscuit, 1758. About 19 cm.*
Wallace Collection, London (Museum photo)

lower left: **56.** Falconet, *Little Girl Hiding Cupid's Bow. Biscuit, 1761. About 19 cm. Victoria and Albert Museum, London (Museum photo)*

upper right: **57.** Falconet, *The Bather with a Sponge. Plaster model, 1762. About 17 cm. Manufacture Nationale de Sèvres (Cliché des Musées Nationaux)*

lower right: **58.** J. Goujon, *Nymph from the "Fontaine des Innocents," ca. 1547-49. Plaster cast (Giraudon)*

59. *Falconet, Fishing.
Plaster model, 1758.
About 27 cm.
Manufacture Nationale de
Sèvres (Cliché des Musées
Nationaux)*

60. *Falconet, The Meat
Cakes. Plaster model,
1759. About 18 cm.
Manufacture Nationale de
Sèvres (Cliché des Musées
Nationaux)*

61. *Falconet, The Given Kiss. Plaster model, 1765. About 28 cm. Manufacture Nationale de Sèvres (Cliché des Musées Nationaux)*

62. *Falconet, The Returned Kiss. Plaster model, 1765. About 28 cm. Manufacture Nationale de Sèvres (Cliché des Musées Nationaux)*

opposite page above: **63.** *Flora with the Quiver of Roses. Probably based on a model by Falconet. About 29.5 cm. Marble, ca. 1750. Cognac-Jay Museum, Paris (Museum photo)*

opposite page below: **64.** *Back view of statuette shown in Fig. 63 (Roger Viollet)*

above: **65.** *Flora with the Quiver of Roses. Probably based on a model by Falconet. Marble, ca. 1750. About 30 cm. Walters Art Gallery, Baltimore (Museum photo)*

left: **66.** *Detail of statuette shown in Fig. 65 (Museum photo)*

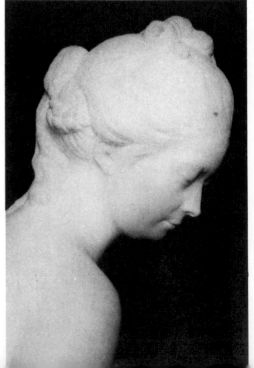

above: **67.** *The Bather with a Towel. Possibly based on a model by Falconet or his followers. Marble, ca. 1770–1780. About 29 cm. Musée des Beaux-Arts, Lons-le-Saunier (Toussaint)*

right: **68.** *Detail of statuette shown in Fig. 67 (Toussaint)*

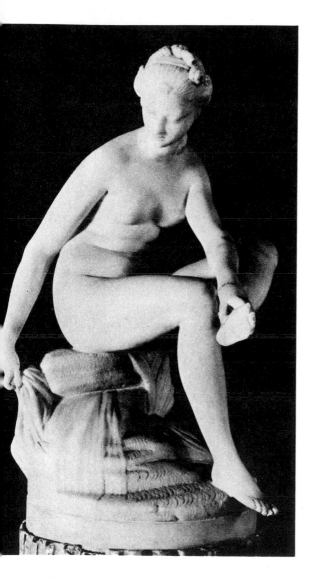

left: **69.** *The Bather with a Towel. Possibly based on a model by Falconet or his followers.*
Marble, ca. 1770–1780. About 25 cm. Cognac-Jay Museum, Paris (Museum photo)

right: **70.** *The Bather with a Towel. Possibly based on a model by Falconet or his followers.*
Marble, ca. 1770–1780. About 27 cm. Waddesdon Manor (Fraser)

upper right: **71.** *Decorated bronze clock. Possibly based on a model by Falconet or his followers. ca. 1770–1780. About 35 cm. Musée de Besançon (Museum photo)*

lower left: **72.** *Venus Nursing Cupid and Venus Chastising Cupid. Possibly based on models by Falconet or his followers. Marble, ca. 1770–1780. About 35 cm. Wallace Collection, London (Museum photo)*

lower right: **73.** *Venus Consoling Cupid. Possibly based on a model by Falconet or his followers. Marble, ca. 1770–1780. About 33 cm. Private collection, Paris (Photo courtesy owner)*

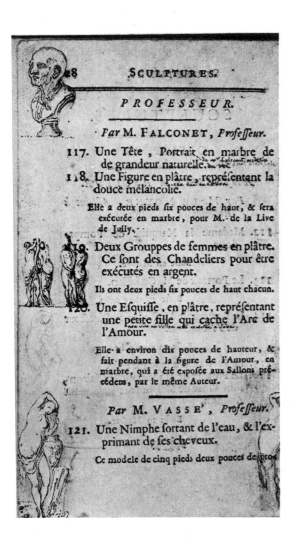

above: 74. G. de Saint-Aubin, Page 28, with sketches of works exhibited, of the "Livret" of the Salon of 1761. Cabinet des Estampes, Bibliothèque Nationale, Paris (Photo Bibl. Nationale)

right: 75. Love Crowned by Fidelity. Possibly based on a model by Falconet or his followers. Marble, ca. 1770–1780. About 50 cm. The Frick Collection, New York (Museum photo)

above: **76.** *Tomb of Louise-Elisabeth La Live de Jully. Anonymous drawing of the tomb designed by Falconet, ca. 1760. Musée Carnavalet, Paris (Museum photo)*

left: **77.** *Falconet, Louise-Elisabeth La Live de Jully. Marble medallion from the destroyed tomb. 1753. Saint-Roch, Paris (Archives Photographiques)*

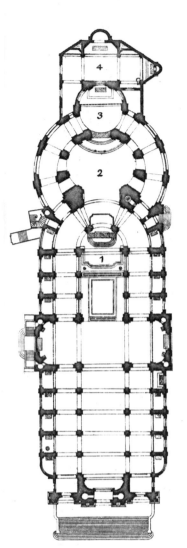

left: **78.** *Plan of Saint-Roch as it appeared after 1754 (date of the addition of the Chapel of the Calvary). 1: Choir. 2: Chapel of the Virgin. 3: Chapel of the Communion. 4: Chapel of the Calvary. Based on a plan in the Bibliothèque du Musée des Arts Décoratifs, Paris*

right: **79.** *C. Norry,* View of the interior of Saint-Roch. *Drawing, ca. 1787. Cabinet des Estampes, Bibliothèque Nationale, Paris (Photo Bibl. Nat.)*

80. *Falconet, Christ in Agony in the Garden of Olives. Stone, ca. 1757–1760. About 190 cm. Saint-Roch, Paris (Bulloz)*

above: 81. *Head of Christ shown in Fig. 8o (Bulloz)*

right: 82. *J. Restout, The Death of Saint Scholastica. Painting, 1730. Musée des Beaux-Arts, Tours (Bulloz)*

left: **83.** *G. L. Bernini, The Ecstasy of Saint Teresa. Marble, 1645–1652. Cornaro Chapel, Santa Maria della Vittoria, Rome (Anderson–Giraudon)*

below: **84.** *Pierre-Etienne Falconet (?), Transportation of the Angel of the Annunciation to Saint–Roch. Drawing for an engraving for Diderot's Encyclopedia, ca. 1758. Musée Carnavalet, Paris (Buchholz)*

85. *View of the interior of Saint-Roch, detail of the drawing
shown in Fig. 79 (Photo Bibliothèque Nationale)*

opposite page: **86.** *Falconet,*
The Glory. Marble and bronze,
ca. 1760. About 17 m. × 10 m.
Saint-Roch, Paris (Bulloz).

right: **87.** *G. L. Bernini, The*
Glory (Cathedra Petri). Marble,
bronze, and stucco, 1657–1666.
St. Peter, Rome (Alinari)

88. *C.-N. Cochin, Phylakei Writing*
against the Glory of Falconet.
Engraving from C.-N. Cochin, Les
Misotechnites aux enfers, Amsterdam,
1763, p. 17. Cabinet des Estampes,
Bibliothèque Nationale, Paris
(Photo Bibliothèque Nationale)

89. *P.-A. de Machy* (?), *View of the Chapel of the Calvary of Saint-Roch.*
Painting, ca. 1768. Musée des Beaux-Arts, Pau (Archives photographiques)

90. *Detail of painting shown in Fig. 89 (Montagne)*

left: **91.** Falconet, *Dr. Camille Falconet at the Age of Seventy-six. Terra-cotta, 1747. Life size.* Musée des Beaux-Arts, Lyons (*Museum photo*)

right: **92.** *Back view of bust shown in Fig. 91 (Museum photo)*

93. *Falconet, Dr. Camille Falconet at the Age of Eighty-nine. Marble, 1760. Life size. Musée des Beaux-Arts, Angers (Evers)*

left: **94.** *Falconet, Madame de Pompadour as Friendship. Biscuit, 1755. About 27 cm. Wadsworth Atheneum, Hartford (Museum photo)*

below: **95.** *Detail of biscuit shown in Fig. 94 (Museum photo)*

97. *Falconet, Peter the Great. Bronze, 1766–1778. View from rider's right. Square of the Decembrists, Leningrad (Ed Clark, Life Magazine)*

98. *Peter the Great. View from rider's left. (Roger Viollet)*

above: **99.** *Marcus Aurelius. Bronze, ca. second century A.D. Campidoglio, Rome (Anderson)*

left: **100.** *Desjardins or Guillaume de Groff (?), Louis XIV. Bronze statuette. First quarter eighteenth century. Michael Hall Fine Arts, Inc., New York (Photo courtesy owner)*

right: 101. F. Girardon, Louis XIV. Small bronze replica of the destroyed statue of Place Vendôme (Place Louis-le-Grand), ca. 1700. Knoedler & Co., New York (Photo courtesy owner)

below: 102. G. L. Bernini, Louis XIV (renamed Marcus Curtius). Marble, 1669–1677. Gardens of the Château de Versailles (Giraudon)

103. *The statue of Peter the Great, with a general view of the Square of the Decembrists and the Neva river (Sovfoto)*

104: *Peter the Great. Small bronze replica (possibly by M.-A. Collot) of Falconet's statue in Leningrad, ca. 1776. Private collection, Holland (Archives Photographiques)*

105. *Head of Horse, detail of Falconet's statue of Peter the Great*

106. *A. Losenko, Drawing of plaster model of Peter the Great statue, 1770. Musée des Beaux-Arts, Nancy (Mangin)*

TETE DE LA STATUE EQUESTRE
DE
PIERRE LE GRAND.

left: 107. B.-L. Henriquez, Head of the Equestrian Statue of Peter the Great. Engraving after a drawing by A. Losenko, 1772 (Roger Viollet)

below: 108. Head of Peter the Great, detail of Falconet's statue (Novosti, courtesy Time, Inc.)

SELECTED BIBLIOGRAPHY

Basic Studies on Falconet's Art

Hildebrandt, E. *Leben, Werke und Schriften des Bildhauers E. M. Falconet.* Strasbourg: Heitz, 1908.

Réau, L. *Etienne-Maurice Falconet.* Paris: Demotte, 1922.

Falconet's Writings

There are four comprehensive editions of his *Oeuvres:* Lausanne, 1781; Paris: Didot, 1785; Paris: Didot and Jombert, 1787; Paris: Dentu, 1808.

Early Biographies

Robin, J.-B.-C. *"Eloge de Falconet, sculpteur."* Extract from *Tribut de la Société nationale des Neuf Soeurs,* Paris, 1791.

Levesque, P.-C. "Vie d'Etienne Falconet." Falconet, *Oeuvres complètes.* Paris: Dentu, 1808, I.

Correspondence

Diderot, Denis. *Oeuvres complètes.* Edited by J. Assézat and M. Tourneux. Paris: Garnier, 1876. XVIII.

Falconet, E.-M. *Correspondance de Falconet avec Catherine II, 1767-1778.* Edited by L. Réau. Paris: Champion, 1921.

Salons

Diderot. *Oeuvres complètes,* X.

Collection de pièces sur les beaux-arts imprimées et manuscrites recueillies par Pierre-Jean Mariette, Charles-Nicolas Cochin et M. Deloynes. Paris, Bibl. Nat., Cabinet des Estampes, I, II, III, IV, V, VI, VII, VIII.

Biscuits

Bourgeois, E. *Le biscuit de Sèvres au XVIIIe siècle.* Paris: 1908.

Verlet, P.; Grandjean, S.; Brunet, M.; *Sèvres.* Paris: le Prot, 1954.

Saint-Roch

"Lettre au sujet des Embellissemens faits dans l'Eglise de S. Roch, avec la Description de ces nouveaux Ouvrages." *Mercure de France,* December, 1760, pp. 148-155.

Diderot. "Observations sur l'église de Saint-Roch." *Oeuvres complètes.* XIII, pp. 4-9.

Falconet in Russia

Zaretskaya, Z. V. *Falconet.* Leningrad: Avrora, 1970.

Peter the Great

Carburi de Ceffalonie (Carburi-Laskary). *Monument élevé à la gloire de Pierre-le-Grand.* Paris: Nyon and Stoupe, 1777.

Arkin, D. *Mednyi Vsadnik.* Leningrad-Moscow: Iskousstvo, 1958.

Falconet's Literary and Aesthetic Significance

Benoit, Y. *Diderot et Falconet: le pour et le contre.* Paris: Les Editeurs Français Réunis, 1958.

Weinshanker, A. B. *Falconet: His Writings and His Friend Diderot.* Geneva: Droz, 1966.

INDEX

Etienne-Maurice Falconet abbreviated as F.   Numbers in italics refer to the illustrations.